FIELD GUIDES

FLOWERS AND PLANTS

Andrea Debbink

Abdo Reference

An Imprint of Abdo Publishing | abdobooks.com

CONTENTS

What Are Flowers and Plants? 4
How to Use This Book 6

Grasses
Big Bluestem 8
Bread Wheat 9
Common Bamboo 10
Common Meadow Grass 11
Common Rice 12
Elephant Grass 13
European Beachgrass 14
Pampas Grass...15

Rushes
Arctic Rush 16
Common Rush 17
Hard Rush 18
Spreading Rush 19

Sedges
Papyrus Sedge 20
Saw Grass 21
Tussock Cottongrass 22
Water Chestnut 23

Other Freshwater Aquatic Plants
Broadleaf Cattail 24
Common Duckweed 25
Sacred Lotus 26
Water Shield 27
White Water Lily 28
Yellow Pond Lily 29

Bromeliads
Pineapple 30
Queen of the Andes 31
Sky Plant 32
Spanish Moss 33

Succulents
Aloe Vera 34
Beavertail Cactus 35
Burro's Tail 36
California Barrel Cactus 37
Common Houseleek 38
Eastern Prickly Pear 39

Wildflowers
Black-Eyed Susan 40
Bloodroot 41
Bluebell 42
Bull Thistle 43
Butterfly Weed 44
Chicory 45
Common Milkweed 46
Common Mullein 47
Common Yellow Wood Sorrel 48
Dandelion 49
Large-Flowered Trillium 50
Oxeye Daisy 51
Pasqueflower 52
Purple Coneflower 53
Queen Anne's Lace 54
Red Columbine 55
Starflower 56
White Clover 57
Wild Leek 58
Yellow Gentian 59

Garden Flowers and Herbs

Common Lilac 60
Common Peony 61
Common Sunflower 62
Dill 63
English Lavender 64
French Marigold 65
Hybrid Tea Rose 66
Impatiens 67
Lily of the Valley 68
Spearmint 69

Vines

Bougainvillea 70
European Ivy 71
Grape Honeysuckle 72
Japanese Wisteria 73
Morning Glory 74
Passion Fruit 75
Star Jasmine 76
Virginia Creeper 77

Berries and Shrubs

American Cranberry 78
Black Raspberry 79
Boxwood 80
Bunchberry 81
Cacao Tree 82
Cloudberry 83
English Holly 84
European Elder 85
Japanese Camellia 86
Lowbush Blueberry 87
Sand Cherry 88
Staghorn Sumac 89
Tea Plant 90
True Indigo 91
Wild Black Currant 92
Wild Strawberry 93

Carnivorous Plants

Common Bladderwort 94
Common Sundew 95
Venus Flytrap 96
Yellow Pitcher Plant 97

Ferns

Bird's-Nest Fern 98
Lady Fern 99
Ostrich Fern 100
Royal Fern 101

Mosses

Bonfire Moss 102
Common Haircap Moss 103
Pincushion Moss 104
Splendid Feather Moss 105

Liverworts

Floating Crystalwort 106
Umbrella Liverwort 107

Glossary 108
To Learn More 109
Photo Credits 110

WHAT ARE FLOWERS AND PLANTS?

A plant is a living thing that makes its own food using photosynthesis. The plant kingdom is incredibly diverse. Plants may have tall trunks or many sturdy stems. Some plants produce flowers while others don't have flowers or seeds at all. Plants can live in nearly every habitat and climate on Earth. Some plants are edible and others are poisonous. Even edible plants can have poisonous look-alikes.

There are many differences between plant species. People categorize plants based on these differences. The two most common groupings are flowering plants and nonflowering plants.

FLOWERING PLANTS

Flowering plants are also called angiosperms. These plants produce flowers that turn into fruits, which contain seeds. Flowers can be colorful and showy, or so small that they're hardly visible. Fruits can be large or fleshy, like apples. Or they can be small and dry, like grains from bread wheat. There are two main types of flowering plants: monocots and eudicots.

- A monocot is a flowering plant that has one cotyledon, the part of the seed that becomes a plant's leaf. Examples of monocots are grasses, rushes, sedges, some freshwater aquatic plants, and bromeliads.

- A eudicot is a flowering plant that has two cotyledons. Examples of eudicots are succulents, wildflowers, garden flowers, herbs, vines, berries, shrubs, and carnivorous plants.

NONFLOWERING PLANTS

Nonflowering plants don't produce flowers or fruits. They reproduce by releasing spores or undergoing vegetative propagation. Vegetative propagation is when new plants grow from parts of parent plants, or when they grow from reproductive structures, such as rhizomes. Some types of nonflowering plants include ferns, mosses, and liverworts.

FLOWER AND PLANT IDENTIFICATION

People can use the following characteristics to help them identify plants:

- Height: Most plants have average heights.

- Stem: Most plants have either woody or herbaceous stems, but some plants don't have stems at all. Woody stems are rigid. They can live for several years and add new growths each year. Herbaceous stems are soft. They last for only one growing season.

- Leaves: The sizes, shapes, colors, and arrangements of leaves can help identify plants.

- Flowers, fruits, and seeds: Plants may produce flowers, fruits, and seeds depending on the seasons. However, not all plants have these things.

- Range: A plant's range is where it is found in the world. Sometimes plants are introduced into non-native areas. They can become invasive.

- Habitat: A plant's habitat is the type of environment it grows in.

- Bloom period: Most plants bloom during specific seasons. They may bloom a few times a year, once a year, or even less frequently than that.

HOW TO USE THIS BOOK

Tab shows the plant category.

OTHER FRESHWATER AQUATIC PLANTS

SACRED LOTUS *(NELUMBO NUCIFERA)*

The sacred lotus is an aquatic plant known for its large, showy flower and its long history with people. These plants ... ical freshwater habitats such as lagoons and ... but they're also popular garden plants. The ... has large, green leaves and a large flower that ... ite in color. The flower rises above the water's ... he plant's stem.

The plant's common name appears here.

HOW TO SPOT

Height: Aquatic
Stem: Herbaceous
Leaves: Rounded, waxy leaves; up to 2 feet (0.6 m) wide
Flowers: Pink or white flowers with yellow centers; 8 to 12 inches (20 to 30 cm) wide
Range: Asia, A... North America ...ltas, lagoons,
Habitat: Fresh... and slow-mov...
Bloom Period:

Images show the plant.

RELIGION AND THE LOTUS

The sacred lotus is important to the Buddhist and Hindu religions. It's seen as a symbol of beauty, purity, and divinity.

Sidebars provide additional information about the topic.

The plant's scientific name appears here.

WATER SHIELD *(BRASENIA SCHREBERI)*

The water shield is a common aquatic plant. It is known for spreading its small, oval-shaped leaves across the surfaces of ponds and lakes. The water shield has a small, compact flower. A thick slime coats the plant's underwater stem and the undersides of its leaves. This slime may protect the water shield from drought and animals.

This paragraph provides information about the plant.

HOW TO SPOT

Height: Aquatic
Stem: Herbaceous
Leaves: Floating, oval-shaped leaves; 1 to 4.5 inches (2.5 to 11 cm) long
Flowers: Small, maroon flowers; 1 inch (2.5 cm) long
Range: Africa, Asia, Australia, North America, Central America, South America, and the Caribbean
Habitat: Ponds, lakes, and slow-moving streams
Bloom Period: Summer

How to Spot boxes give information on how to identify the plant.

FUN FACT
The water shield is a food source for waterfowl.

Fun Facts give interesting information related to the plant.

27

GRASSES

BIG BLUESTEM
(ANDROPOGON GERARDII)

Big bluestems are tall perennial grasses. They once dominated in North American prairies. These grasses can still be found in prairie habitats, and they are also used as ornamental plants in landscaping. They thrive in full sun, and their complex root systems help them survive droughts. Big bluestems are bunchgrasses. That means they grow in large clumps.

HOW TO SPOT

Height: 4 to 6 feet (1.2 to 1.8 m)

Stem: Herbaceous

Leaves: Clusters of flattened leaves; up to 2 inches (5 cm) long and 3.8 inches (9.7 cm) wide

Flowers: Purplish flower clusters; up to 4 inches (10 cm) long

Range: North America

Habitat: Prairies or fields in full sun

Bloom Period: Fall and winter

GRASSES

There are more than 10,000 grass species, and they can grow in many habitats. Grasses are flowering plants. They have hollow, round stems that are jointed, or broken into segments. They also have far-reaching root systems and can have long, blade-like leaves.

BREAD WHEAT *(TRITICUM AESTIVUM)*

Bread wheat is an annual domesticated grass that is grown for its fruit, or grain. The grains are either ground or used whole to make foods such as flour, breakfast cereals, and pasta noodles. Bread wheat is a bunchgrass with a hollow stem. Long, thin leaves grow around the stem in a whorl.

HOW TO SPOT

Height: Up to 4 feet (1.2 m)
Stem: Herbaceous
Leaves: Narrow leaves; 7 to 15 inches (18 to 38 cm) long and 0.5 inches (1.3 cm) wide
Flowers: Overlapping spikelets; 2 to 4 inches (5 to 10 cm) long
Range: Worldwide
Habitat: Sunny fields in temperate climates
Bloom Period: Fall and winter

FUN FACT
Bread wheat is also known as common wheat. It's one of the most important food crops in the world.

GRASSES

COMMON BAMBOO
(BAMBUSA VULGARIS)

There are more than 1,000 species of bamboo. Common bamboo is among the largest and fastest growing. These tree-like grasses grow in clumps of tall, hollow shoots. The plants produce green compound leaves with thin leaflets. The smooth, above-ground stems are divided into segments. They sprout from an underground stem called a rhizome. Common bamboos rarely produce flowers.

HOW TO SPOT

Height: Up to 65 feet (20 m)
Stem: Woody
Leaves: Compound leaves with several narrow leaflets; up to 12 inches (30 cm) long
Flowers: Uncommon
Range: Asia, Africa, Australia, North America, and South America
Habitat: Moist, tropical forests
Bloom Period: Rare

BAMBOO'S USES

Bamboo is an incredibly useful plant. Its young shoots are edible, and parts of the plant can be used for medicinal purposes. Bamboo is also used worldwide as a building material for things such as flooring, tool handles, fences, and furniture. It can even be used to make clothing.

COMMON MEADOW GRASS
(POA PRATENSIS)

Common meadow grass is native to most of Europe and northern Asia, and it's found throughout North America. Also known as Kentucky bluegrass, it's one of the most popular lawn grasses in the United States. That's because common meadow grass is a turfgrass. That means its many green blades form a dense, thick mat.

HOW TO SPOT

Height: 1 to 4 inches (2.5 to 10 cm) on lawns; up to 3 feet (0.9 m) in the wild

Stem: Herbaceous

Leaves: Long, narrow leaves; up to 8 inches (20 cm) long and 0.2 inches (0.5 cm) wide

Flowers: Clusters of spikelets that are light to purplish green; 2 to 8 inches (5 to 20 cm) long

Range: Europe, northern Asia, and North America

Habitat: Fields and lawns in cool, temperate climates

Bloom Period: Late spring to early summer

FUN FACT
When common meadow grass grows to its natural height of 3 feet (0.9 m), it produces colorful spikelet clusters.

GRASSES

COMMON RICE *(ORYZA SATIVA)*

Common rice is sometimes called Asian rice, and it's one of the most popular rice species. While it's no longer found in the wild, people grow it in fields and hillsides as a food crop. Common rice, like all rice varieties, produces long, spike-like clusters of flowers that eventually become grains. These grains are the rice that people eat.

FUN FACT
There are three main categories of rice: long, medium, and short.

HOW TO SPOT

Height: Up to 4 feet (1.2 m)
Stem: Herbaceous
Leaves: Long, flat leaves
Flowers: Long spikelets of tiny flowers
Range: Africa, Asia, Australia, Europe, North America, and South America
Habitat: Cultivated fields in the tropics and subtropics
Bloom Period: Variable

AN ANCIENT, IMPORTANT CROP

Rice is an ancient crop. There's archaeological evidence that people grew it in China between 7000 and 5000 BCE. Today, rice is the main food source for half the world's population.

ELEPHANT GRASS
(PENNISETUM PURPUREUM)

Elephant grass is a tall, perennial plant that's also known as Napier grass. Elephant grasses grow in clumps of thin, upright stems. They have very long, narrow leaves. Elephant grasses produce cylindrical-shaped clusters made of many tiny flowers. The flower clusters are greenish tan and have feathery and bristly appearances.

HOW TO SPOT

Height: Up to 15 feet (4.6 m)
Stem: Herbaceous
Leaves: Flat, strap-like leaves that are several feet long
Flowers: Greenish-tan, cylindrical-shaped clusters with tiny flower spikelets; 5 to 12 inches (12.7 to 30 cm) long
Range: Asia, Africa, Australia, Europe, North America, and South America
Habitat: Swamps and lowlands
Bloom Period: Fall

GRASSES

EUROPEAN BEACHGRASS
(AMMOPHILA ARENARIA)

European beachgrass is a tall perennial grass. It grows along sandy beaches throughout the world, but it is native to Europe and western Asia. As a bunchgrass, it grows in a large clump that can be nearly 4 feet (1.2 m) tall. European beachgrasses grow from rhizomes. These are large, underground plant stems that anchor the grasses into the sand.

HOW TO SPOT

Height: Nearly 4 feet (1.2 m)
Stem: Herbaceous
Leaves: Clusters of flattened leaves; up to 2 feet (0.6 m) long and 3.8 inches (9.7 cm) wide
Flowers: Whitish flower clusters; up to 1 foot (0.3 m) long
Range: Asia, Europe, and North America
Habitat: Sand dunes
Bloom Period: Spring and summer

NATIVE, NON-NATIVE, AND INVASIVE

Plants are often described as being native, non-native, or invasive. A native plant originated in the location being described. A non-native plant was introduced to a specific location, usually by people. An invasive plant can be native or non-native. It causes harm to the ecosystem where it lives. For example, European beachgrass is a native plant in Europe but an invasive species in North America, where it crowds out native plants.

PAMPAS GRASS
(CORTADERIA SELLOANA)

Pampas grass is originally from South America. Today, people have pampas grasses in lawns and gardens throughout the world. These plants grow in dense clumps, and their leaves and flowers give them dramatic appearances. Their thin, serrated leaves bend in graceful arches. In the fall, the plants produce flowers that look like feathery plumes.

HOW TO SPOT

Height: Up to 9 feet (2.7 m)
Stem: Herbaceous
Leaves: Sharp-edged, narrow leaves; 6 to 8 feet (1.8 to 2.4 m) long
Flowers: Silver-white, feathery plumes; 1 to 3 feet (0.3 to 0.9 m) long
Range: Africa, Australia, Europe, North America, and South America
Habitat: Fields, lawns, and gardens
Bloom Period: Early fall to winter

FUN FACT
Pampas is the name for the South American grasslands east of the Andes Mountains.

RUSHES

ARCTIC RUSH *(JUNCUS ARCTICUS)*

Rushes look like grasses, but they have round, solid stems instead of hollow stems like grasses. Arctic rush plants produce several dark-green stems that grow straight and tall. Arctic rushes don't have leaves, but they do have brownish-purple flowers that grow directly from the stems. This plant is also known as Baltic rush.

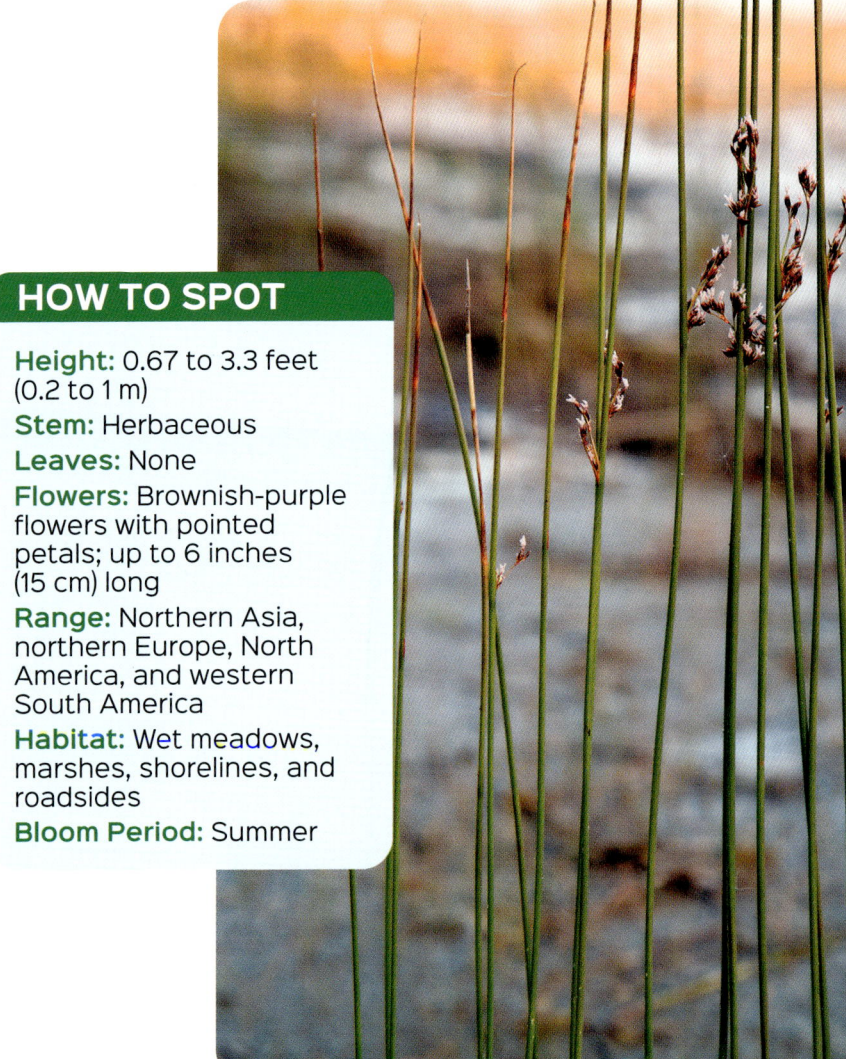

HOW TO SPOT

Height: 0.67 to 3.3 feet (0.2 to 1 m)

Stem: Herbaceous

Leaves: None

Flowers: Brownish-purple flowers with pointed petals; up to 6 inches (15 cm) long

Range: Northern Asia, northern Europe, North America, and western South America

Habitat: Wet meadows, marshes, shorelines, and roadsides

Bloom Period: Summer

COMMON RUSH *(JUNCUS EFFUSUS)*

Common rushes are grass-like plants that grow in clumps of thin, leafless stems. The stems are green and smooth. Although they look stiff, they're soft to the touch. After the plant's flowers die and produce seeds in the fall, the common rush turns yellow, then brown.

HOW TO SPOT

Height: Up to 4 feet (1.2 m)
Stem: Herbaceous
Leaves: None
Flowers: Loose clusters of tiny, yellowish-green or pale-brown flowers; flowers are less than 1 inch (2.5 cm) wide
Range: Asia, Australia, Europe, and North America
Habitat: Swamps, marshes, riverbanks, shorelines, and wet pastures
Bloom Period: Summer

RUSHES

HARD RUSH *(JUNCUS INFLEXUS)*

Hard rushes thrive in moist soils and freshwater habitats. These plants can grow in standing water that's up to 3 feet (0.9 m) deep. The rhizomes of hard rushes sprout cylindrical, blue-green stems that grow upright and tall. In the late spring, some of the stems produce flower clusters.

HOW TO SPOT

Height: Up to around 3 feet (0.9 m)

Stem: Herbaceous

Leaves: None

Flowers: Loose clusters of tiny, reddish-brown flowers

Range: Asia, northern Africa, Europe, and North America

Habitat: Wet meadows, marshes, and shorelines

Bloom Period: Late spring to summer

SPREADING RUSH *(JUNCUS PATENS)*

The spreading rush is also called the California gray rush. These plants grow in dense clumps of cylindrical stems. The stems are gray green and leafless. From spring through fall, some of the stems produce golden-brown flowers. Although the spreading rush is native to North America and can be found in the wild, it's also often grown as a garden plant.

FUN FACT
Spreading rushes are also called wire grasses because of their thin, leafless stems.

HOW TO SPOT

Height: Up to 2 feet (0.6 m)
Stem: Herbaceous
Leaves: None
Flowers: Loose clusters of small, golden-brown flowers
Range: North America
Habitat: Shaded gardens, fields, and shorelines
Bloom Period: Spring and fall

SEDGES

PAPYRUS SEDGE *(CYPERUS PAPYRUS)*

Papyrus sedges thrive in water. They grow in dense clumps spread along the ground. Like all plants in this family, papyrus sedges have solid, triangular stems. They don't have leaves, but the tops of the stems produce growths that looks like feather dusters. Flowers bloom at the ends of these thread-like stems.

FUN FACT
People in ancient Egypt used papyrus sedge stems to make an early form of paper called papyrus.

HOW TO SPOT

Height: Up to 15 feet (4.6 m)
Stem: Herbaceous
Leaves: None
Flowers: Tiny, greenish-brown flowers
Range: Africa, Europe, and North America
Habitat: Marshes, riverbanks, and shorelines
Bloom Period: Summer and fall

SAW GRASS *(CLADIUM JAMAICENSE)*

Despite having *grass* in its name, saw grass is a species of sedge. Saw grasses are usually found in wet habitats, such as tropical marshes and swamps, but they can also grow in drier soils. The plant gets its name from its sharp-edged leaves.

HOW TO SPOT

Height: 7 feet (2 m)
Stem: Herbaceous
Leaves: Stiff, narrow leaves with serrated edges; up to 3 feet (0.9 m) long
Flowers: Large, drooping clusters of brown spikelets; 12 to 20 inches (30 to 50 cm) long
Range: North America, Central America, and South America
Habitat: Freshwater and brackish wetlands and shorelines
Bloom Period: Spring and summer

SEDGES, GRASSES, AND RUSHES

Sedges are grass-like plants that are easy to mistake for grasses or rushes. One way to tell if a plant is a sedge is to feel its stem. The cross section of a sedge stem is usually triangular and has edges that can be felt when rolled between the fingers, unlike a grass or rush. Sedges also tend to have branches and solid stems rather than hollow ones.

SEDGES

TUSSOCK COTTONGRASS
(ERIOPHORUM VAGINATUM)

Tussock cottongrasses are common sedges found in the northern parts of the northern hemisphere, especially in wet habitats such as swamps and bogs. These plants grow in dense clumps of triangular stems. The clumps are called tussocks. They are made up of cottongrass roots and old stems that have died. At the top of each stem is a feathery flower cluster. It looks like a rabbit's tail, which is why tussock cottongrass is sometimes called hare's-tail cottongrass.

HOW TO SPOT

Height: Up to 2 feet (0.6 m)
Stem: Herbaceous
Leaves: None
Flowers: Dense clusters of feathery flowers; up to 2 inches (5 cm) long
Range: Asia, Europe, North America, and the Arctic
Habitat: Wet meadows, swamps, and tundra
Bloom Period: Summer

WATER CHESTNUT
(ELEOCHARIS DULCIS)

Water chestnuts grow in shallow waters and along swamps, ponds, and lakes. They're known for producing edible underground vegetables that are also called water chestnuts. These plants have thin, leafless stems and can have yellow-brown flower spikelets.

HOW TO SPOT

Height: Up to 3 feet (0.9 m)
Stem: Herbaceous
Leaves: None
Flowers: Cylindrical, yellow-brown flower spikelets; up to 2 inches (5 cm) long
Range: Asia, Australia, and North America
Habitat: In or along ponds, swamps, and lakes
Bloom Period: Summer and fall

FUN FACT
A water chestnut vegetable can be eaten raw or cooked. It has a slightly sweet flavor and a crunchy texture.

OTHER FRESHWATER AQUATIC PLANTS

BROADLEAF CATTAIL
(TYPHA LATIFOLIA)

The broadleaf cattail is also known as the common cattail. These plants are found in freshwater wetlands throughout the world. Broadleaf cattails grow along the edges of swamps and marshes in shallow waters up to 1 foot (0.3 m) deep. The upper part of the cattail's flower pollinates the lower half. When these seeds mature, they become soft fruits that are shaped like hot dogs.

HOW TO SPOT

Height: 4 to 6 feet (1.2 to 1.8 m)
Stem: Herbaceous
Leaves: Narrow, sword-like leaves; 7 inches (18 cm) long
Flowers: Dense, cylinder-shaped spikes; 6 to 10 inches (15 to 25 cm) long
Range: Northern Africa, northern and central Asia, Europe, and North America
Habitat: Wetlands
Bloom Period: Summer

COMMON DUCKWEED *(LEMNA MINOR)*

Common duckweed often looks like a bright-green, carpet-like growth on the surface of ponds or lakes. The growth is made up of hundreds of common duckweed plants. Each plant has just one small leaf that floats on the water's surface while a small root hangs below. Duckweeds have microscopic flowers, yet pollinators such as bees are still able to find them.

FUN FACT
Duckweeds are the smallest known flowering plants. They're a popular food among many aquatic animals, including ducks, which give the plants their name.

HOW TO SPOT

Height: Aquatic
Stem: Herbaceous
Leaves: Single oval leaf; up to 0.25 inches (0.64 cm) long
Flowers: Microscopic
Range: Africa, Asia, Europe, and North America
Habitat: Freshwater ponds and lakes
Bloom Period: Summer

OTHER FRESHWATER AQUATIC PLANTS

SACRED LOTUS *(NELUMBO NUCIFERA)*

The sacred lotus is an aquatic plant known for its large, showy flower and its long history with people. These plants grow in tropical freshwater habitats such as lagoons and river deltas, but they're also popular garden plants. The sacred lotus has large, green leaves and a large flower that is pink or white in color. The flower rises above the water's surface on the plant's stem.

HOW TO SPOT

Height: Aquatic
Stem: Herbaceous
Leaves: Rounded, waxy leaves; up to 2 feet (0.6 m) wide
Flowers: Pink or white flowers with yellow centers; 8 to 12 inches (20 to 30 cm) wide
Range: Asia, Australia, and North America
Habitat: Freshwater ponds, lakes, river deltas, lagoons, and slow-moving streams
Bloom Period: Summer

RELIGION AND THE LOTUS

The sacred lotus is important to the Buddhist and Hindu religions. It's seen as a symbol of beauty, purity, and divinity.

WATER SHIELD *(BRASENIA SCHREBERI)*

The water shield is a common aquatic plant. It is known for spreading its small, oval-shaped leaves across the surfaces of ponds and lakes. The water shield has a small, compact flower. A thick slime coats the plant's underwater stem and the undersides of its leaves. This slime may protect the water shield from drought and animals.

HOW TO SPOT

Height: Aquatic
Stem: Herbaceous
Leaves: Floating, oval-shaped leaves; 1 to 4.5 inches (2.5 to 11 cm) long
Flowers: Small, maroon flowers; 1 inch (2.5 cm) long
Range: Africa, Asia, Australia, North America, Central America, South America, and the Caribbean
Habitat: Ponds, lakes, and slow-moving streams
Bloom Period: Summer

FUN FACT
The water shield is a food source for waterfowl.

OTHER FRESHWATER AQUATIC PLANTS

WHITE WATER LILY
(NYMPHAEA ODORATA)

White water lilies are aquatic plants that float on the surfaces of still ponds and lakes. Sometimes they're found in slow-moving streams. The plant's stem is rooted in mud at the bottom of the body of water. The lily's leaves are sometimes called lily pads. The leaves are large, shiny, and green. The plant's cup-like flower is white with many pointed petals and a yellow center.

HOW TO SPOT

Height: Aquatic

Stem: Herbaceous

Leaves: Smooth leaves that are round or heart-shaped; 6 to 12 inches (15 to 30 cm) wide

Flowers: White flowers with pointed petals and yellow centers; 3 to 6 inches (7.6 to 15 cm) wide

Range: North America

Habitat: Freshwater ponds, lakes, and streams

Bloom Period: Summer

YELLOW POND LILY *(NUPHAR LUTEA)*

Like other water lilies, yellow pond lilies have leaves and flowers that float on the water's surface. They also have underwater stems that grow up from the mud below. However, the yellow pond lily can grow in deeper water than other lily species. That's because the yellow lily's stem can grow up to 6 feet (1.8 m) tall. In the summer, yellow pond lilies have rounded, cup-shaped, yellow flowers that open in the morning and close at night.

FUN FACT
There are more than 50 water lily species.

HOW TO SPOT

Height: Aquatic
Stem: Herbaceous
Leaves: Smooth leaves that are round or heart-shaped; 3 to 8 inches (7.6 to 20 cm) long
Flowers: Yellow, cup-shaped flowers; 2 inches (5 cm) wide
Range: Africa, Asia, Europe, North America, and the Caribbean
Habitat: Freshwater ponds and lakes
Bloom Period: Summer and fall

BROMELIADS

PINEAPPLE *(ANANAS COMOSUS)*

Pineapples have pointed succulent leaves that grow in rosettes. These plants produce clusters of purple or burgundy flowers that grow on long stalks. A cluster will eventually become the plant's fruit, a pineapple. A single pineapple plant only produces one pineapple. Before it dies, the plant creates other pineapple plants by spreading its small shoots, called suckers.

HOW TO SPOT

Height: 3 to 4 feet (0.9 to 1.2 m)
Stem: Herbaceous
Leaves: Pointed, spiny-edged leaves; 3 feet (0.9 m) long or more
Flowers: Clusters of purple or burgundy flowers on long stalks; flowers are less than 1 inch (2.5 cm) long
Fruits: Rough, oval-shaped fruits; up to 1 foot (0.3 m) long
Range: South America, South Africa, Asia, Hawaii, and southern Florida
Habitat: Cultivated fields and gardens
Bloom Period: Seasonal

FUN FACT
It is possible to grow a pineapple indoors, but the fruit doesn't get as large or taste as sweet as a pineapple grown outside.

QUEEN OF THE ANDES
(PUYA RAIMONDII)

The queen of the Andes is the largest bromeliad in the world, growing up to 30 feet (9 m) tall. It's also very rare, living only in the Andes Mountains and in some botanical gardens. The queen of the Andes has long, spike-like leaves that grow in a spherical pattern. After living for decades, the plant produces a single tall stalk that has thousands of white flowers.

HOW TO SPOT

Height: Up to 30 feet (9 m)
Stem: Herbaceous
Leaves: Long, spike-like leaves; 9 to 13 feet (2.7 to 4 m) long
Flowers: Thousands of white flowers on a tall central stalk
Range: South America
Habitat: Mountains
Bloom Period: Once in the plant's lifetime

BROMELIADS

SKY PLANT *(TILLANDSIA IONANTHA)*

The sky plant is a type of air plant—a species that doesn't need to be in soil to grow. Instead, it gets its moisture and nutrients from the rain and air. In the wild, air plants often grow on other plants, including trees. Sky plants have succulent leaves that usually grow in rosettes. The inner leaves often turn red before sky plants produce bluish-purple, spike-like flowers.

HOW TO SPOT

Height: 6 to 12 inches (15 to 30 cm)
Stem: Herbaceous
Leaves: Narrow, blade-shaped leaves; 1 to 3 inches (2.5 to 7.6 cm) long
Flowers: Bluish-purple, spike-like flowers; 1 inch (2.5 cm) wide
Range: North America, Central America, and South America
Habitat: Tropical and subtropical areas
Bloom Period: Each season

WHAT ARE BROMELIADS?

Air plants are a type of bromeliad. Bromeliads are a group of evergreen perennial plants that usually have succulent-like leaves growing in spirals. Some bromeliads, such as air plants, are epiphytes. That means they grow on other plants and get their nutrients from the air. Other bromeliads, such as pineapples, are terrestrial. That means they grow in the ground.

SPANISH MOSS
(TILLANDSIA USNEOIDES)

Spanish moss is not actually a type of moss but a species of bromeliad. As an air plant, Spanish moss doesn't have roots. It grows by attaching itself to a tree and sometimes to a human-made structure, such as a fence. These plants appear in dense, drooping clumps of tiny, greenish-gray evergreen leaves.

HOW TO SPOT

Height: 3 to 20 feet (0.9 to 6 m)
Stem: Woody
Leaves: Needle-like evergreen leaves; 1 to 3 inches (2.5 to 7.6 cm) long
Flowers: A single blue-green, spike-like flower; less than 1 inch (2.5 cm) long
Range: North America and South America
Habitat: Trees in humid environments that are near water
Bloom Period: Summer and fall

FUN FACT
Because of its appearance, Spanish moss is sometimes called old man's beard.

SUCCULENTS

ALOE VERA *(ALOE BARBADENSIS)*

Aloe vera is an evergreen succulent. These popular garden plants are best known for the juices inside their leaves, also called aloe. Aloe vera plants grow in large clumps of long, fleshy leaves that form rosettes. The leaves are light green and have sharp, spiny edges and pointed tips. In winter, aloe vera can produce a reddish flower that blooms on a stalk in the center of the plant.

HOW TO SPOT

Height: 1 to 2 feet (0.3 to 0.6 m)
Stem: Succulent
Leaves: Fleshy, spiny-edged leaves with pointed ends; 1.5 to 3 feet (0.45 to 0.9 m) long
Flowers: Reddish flowers; up to 3 inches (7.6 cm) long
Range: Africa, Asia, Australia, Europe, North America, and the Middle East
Habitat: Dry forests, shrublands, and gardens
Bloom Period: Winter

FUN FACT
The juices inside aloe vera leaves have long been used to treat skin conditions such as sunburns.

BEAVERTAIL CACTUS
(OPUNTIA BASILARIS)

The beavertail cactus is a species of prickly pear cactus. A single plant can be made up of hundreds of flat, fleshy stem segments that are shaped like beaver tails. The beavertail cactus doesn't have long spines, but it does have many short, sharp bristles. In spring, the cactus produces bright magenta flowers.

HOW TO SPOT

Height: 6 to 12 inches (15 to 30 cm)
Stem: Succulent
Leaves: None
Flowers: Magenta flowers; 2 to 3 inches (5 to 7.6 cm) wide
Range: Mexico and the southwestern United States
Habitat: Deserts
Bloom Period: Spring

SUCCULENTS

BURRO'S TAIL *(SEDUM MORGANIANUM)*

Burro's tail is an evergreen succulent that's native to Mexico and Central America, though it's a popular houseplant throughout the world. These plants have long, trailing stems covered in many small, fragile, bean-shaped leaves that can be easily broken off. In the summer, burro's tails produce clusters of red or pink flowers at the ends of their stems.

HOW TO SPOT

Height: 2 feet (0.6 m)
Stem: Succulent
Leaves: Fleshy, bean-shaped leaves; less than 1 inch (2.5 cm) long
Flowers: Clusters of red or pink flowers; less than 1 inch (2.5 cm) long
Range: North America and Central America
Habitat: Dry environments
Bloom Period: Summer

CALIFORNIA BARREL CACTUS
(FEROCACTUS CYLINDRACEUS)

The California barrel cactus grows in a rounded, cylindrical shape that looks like a barrel. Its shape can also be spherical. When these cacti are young, they're covered in long red spines. The spines turn gray as the plants age. California barrel cacti produce yellow flowers with red or yellow centers.

HOW TO SPOT

Height: 6.6 to 10 feet (2 to 3 m)
Stem: Succulent
Leaves: None
Flowers: Cup-shaped, yellow flowers with red or yellow centers; up to 2.3 inches (6 cm) wide
Range: North America
Habitat: Deserts and rocky and sandy soils
Bloom Period: Spring

FUN FACT
The California barrel cactus can live to be 100 years old.

SUCCULENTS

COMMON HOUSELEEK
(SEMPERVIVUM TECTORUM)

The common houseleek is a compact succulent. It's native to southern Europe, where it grows in sandy or rocky soil. Houseleeks have fleshy, light-green, pointed leaves that form several layers of rosettes. One common houseleek can produce many rosettes, forming a mat along the ground. It's a popular house and garden plant.

FUN FACT
The common houseleek is also called hens and chicks. That's because each mature plant, known as the hen, can produce offshoots that grow new plants known as chicks.

HOW TO SPOT

Height: 6 to 12 inches (15 to 30 cm)
Stem: Succulent
Leaves: Rosettes can be up to 4 inches (10 cm) wide with 50 to 60 fleshy leaves
Flowers: Reddish-purple flower clusters on stems that can grow 12 inches (30 cm) tall
Range: Europe and North America
Habitat: Mountains and gardens
Bloom Period: Summer

EASTERN PRICKLY PEAR
(OPUNTIA HUMIFUSA)

Eastern prickly pears are flowering cacti known for their beautiful, yellowish-orange flowers. These plants are divided into several fleshy green segments and are covered in short bristles and long spikes. Eastern prickly pears can grow along the ground or become upright shrubs.

HOW TO SPOT

Height: 2 feet (0.6 m)
Stem: Succulent
Leaves: None
Flowers: Multiple yellowish-orange flowers; 2 to 3 inches (5 to 7.6 cm) wide
Range: North America
Habitat: Sandy and rocky soils
Bloom Period: Spring and summer

WILDFLOWERS

BLACK-EYED SUSAN
(RUDBECKIA HIRTA)

A black-eyed Susan can have several stems, and each stem has a single flower. The flower's yellow petals radiate from its center. The cone-shaped center of this prairie wildflower appears black or brown from a distance, but it's actually a very dark purple.

HOW TO SPOT

Height: 1 to 3 feet (0.3 to 0.9 m)
Stem: Herbaceous
Leaves: Narrow, smooth-edged leaves with hairy surfaces; 2 to 7 inches (5 to 18 cm) long
Flowers: Yellow, disk-shaped flowers with dark-purple centers; 2 to 3 inches (5 to 7.6 cm) wide
Range: North America
Habitat: Prairies, fields, and deciduous forests
Bloom Period: Summer and fall

BLOODROOT *(SANGUINARIA CANADENSIS)*

Bloodroot is a woodland flower that blooms in early spring. Each plant has several large, lobed leaves and a single flower. The flower is usually white, but it can also be pink. It has several pointed petals radiating from a yellow center. The flower opens in the morning and closes at night.

FUN FACT
Bloodroots have leaves and roots that contain red-orange juices. That's how the plant got its name.

HOW TO SPOT

Height: 4 to 8 inches (10 to 20 cm)
Stem: Herbaceous
Leaves: Large, rounded leaves with five to nine lobes; 4 to 7 inches (10 to 18 cm) wide
Flowers: White or pink flowers with eight or more petals and yellow centers; 2 inches (5 cm) wide
Range: North America
Habitat: Deciduous woods
Bloom Period: Spring

WILDFLOWERS

BLUEBELL *(CAMPANULA ROTUNDIFOLIA)*

Bluebells can grow in challenging environments, such as on mountainsides or along rivers or streams. The flowers can be blue or purple, and they are shaped like tiny bells. They droop from thin stalks. Each bell is made up of five petals that are connected along their sides. These wildflowers grow in small patches.

HOW TO SPOT

Height: 6 to 20 inches (15 to 51 cm)

Stem: Herbaceous

Leaves: Thin, grass-like leaves; 3 inches (7.6 cm) long

Flowers: Pale blue or purple bell-shaped flowers; 0.75 inches (1.9 cm) long

Range: Europe and North America

Habitat: Rocky slopes, riverbanks, and meadows

Bloom Period: Summer

BULL THISTLE *(CIRSIUM VULGARE)*

The bull thistle is the largest species in the thistle family. Thistles are a group of flowering plants that have sharp spines. The bull thistle has the most spines of any thistle. The stems, leaves, and blossoms are all covered by spines. Despite their spiky appearance, these plants have reddish-purple flowers that attract many pollinators, such as bees.

HOW TO SPOT

Height: 2 to 6 feet (0.6 to 1.8 m)

Stem: Herbaceous

Leaves: Narrow, lobed leaves; up to 7 inches (18 cm) long

Flowers: Reddish-purple flowers on spiky green bases; 1.5 to 2 inches (3.8 to 5 cm) wide

Range: Western Asia, northwestern Africa, Europe, and North America

Habitat: Fields, pastures, and roadsides

Bloom Period: Summer and fall

FUN FACT

The bull thistle is an invasive species in North America. It spreads easily, and it quickly grows to a large size. It can outcompete native plants for resources.

WILDFLOWERS

BUTTERFLY WEED
(ASCLEPIAS TUBEROSA)

The butterfly weed is a cousin to the common milkweed. In fact, another name for the butterfly weed is orange milkweed. Butterfly weeds grow in clumps on prairies and disturbed areas such as roadsides and railroad tracks. People also plant butterfly weeds in their gardens to attract butterflies. The bright-orange flowers grow in clusters at the tops of the plants. They become seedpods in the fall.

HOW TO SPOT

Height: 1 to 3 feet (0.3 to 0.9 m)
Stem: Herbaceous
Leaves: Long, pointed leaves with wide bases; 2 to 6 inches (5 to 15 cm) long
Flowers: Flat clusters of small, orange flowers; 2 inches (5 cm) wide
Range: North America
Habitat: Prairies and meadows with sandy soils
Bloom Period: Spring and summer

FUN FACT
Butterfly weed is a species of milkweed. It is one of the host plants for monarch butterfly caterpillars.

CHICORY *(CICHORIUM INTYBUS)*

Chicories are wildflowers that thrive in disturbed areas, such as along roadsides or cultivated fields. Chicories have several small, violet-blue flowers along their stems. The flower petals have fringed ends.

HOW TO SPOT

Height: 2 to 6 feet (0.6 to 1.8 m)
Stem: Herbaceous
Leaves: Long, toothed leaves; 3 to 6 inches (7.6 to 15 cm) long
Flowers: Disk-shaped flowers with violet-blue petals; 1.5 inches (3.8 cm) wide
Range: Asia, Australia, Europe, and North America
Habitat: Sunny fields and roadsides
Bloom Period: Summer and fall

THE CHICORY ROOT

The chicory has a long main root called a taproot. It reaches deep into the ground and can be harvested for cooking purposes. The root can be roasted and ground up. Some people add it to coffee. Others brew it to make a bitter drink similar to coffee.

WILDFLOWERS

COMMON MILKWEED
(ASCLEPIAS SYRIACA)

Common milkweeds grow in fields and along roadsides. In the summer, milkweeds have clusters of pinkish-purple flowers. They also have large, oval-shaped leaves with fuzzy undersides. In the fall, the plants have bumpy seedpods. These open and release many brown seeds attached to fluffy, white hairs.

HOW TO SPOT

Height: 2 to 6 feet (0.6 to 1.8 m)
Stem: Herbaceous
Leaves: Large, smooth, oval leaves; 6 to 8 inches (15 to 20 cm) long
Flowers: Round clusters of pinkish-purple flowers; 2 inches (5 cm) wide
Range: North America
Habitat: Prairies, fields, and roadsides
Bloom Period: Summer

COMMON MILKWEEDS AND BUTTERFLIES

Common milkweeds are food sources for more than 450 insects. This includes North America's monarch butterflies. Monarch butterfly caterpillars eat only milkweed plants.

COMMON MULLEIN
(VERBASCUM THAPSUS)

Common mulleins are biennial plants. That means they only bloom about every two years. In their first year, these plants have rosettes of leaves that grow close to the ground. By their second year, mulleins are tall, narrow plants. They have large leaves that point upward and spike-shaped clusters of small flowers.

HOW TO SPOT

Height: 2 to 7 feet (0.6 to 2 m)

Stem: Herbaceous

Leaves: Large leaves covered in soft hairs; 6 to 15 inches (15 to 38 cm) long

Flowers: Spike-shaped clusters that are 1.6 feet (0.48 m) long and consist of many small, yellow flowers

Range: Asia, Europe, and North America

Habitat: Dry fields and meadows with stony soils

Bloom Period: Summer and fall

FUN FACT
Another name for the common mullein is the flannel plant. That's due to its very soft leaves. They feel like flannel fabric.

WILDFLOWERS

COMMON YELLOW WOOD SORREL *(OXALIS STRICTA)*

The common yellow wood sorrel has a long taproot that grows deep into the ground. Above ground, wood sorrels produce many stems that can grow upright or spread along the ground. Yellow flowers usually bloom from spring to fall. However, in some parts of the common yellow wood sorrels' range, their flowers bloom year-round.

FUN FACT
The common yellow wood sorrel's compound, heart-shaped leaf is also known as a shamrock.

HOW TO SPOT

Height: Up to 9 inches (23 cm)
Stem: Herbaceous
Leaves: Compound leaves with three heart-shaped leaflets; 0.75 to 1 inch (1.9 to 2.5 cm) wide
Flowers: Small, yellow flowers with five distinct petals; 0.4 inches (1 cm) wide
Range: North America
Habitat: Open forests, fields, lawns, and gardens
Bloom Period: Spring and fall or year-round

DANDELION *(TARAXACUM OFFICINALE)*

Today, many people view dandelions as weeds. These adaptable flowers were first brought to the Americas as food plants and were a common sight in eastern North America by the mid-1600s. Their familiar yellow flowers start blooming in early spring and soon transform into fuzzy, globe-shaped seed heads. Dandelions can bloom several times throughout a growing season.

HOW TO SPOT

Height: 8 to 12 inches (20 to 30 cm)
Stem: Herbaceous
Leaves: Toothed and lobed leaves; 3 to 6 inches (7.6 to 15 cm) long
Flowers: Yellow, disk-shaped flowers; 1 to 3 inches (2.5 to 7.6 cm) wide
Range: Southern Africa, Asia, Europe, North America, and South America
Habitat: Sunny fields and lawns
Bloom Period: Spring

THE LION'S TOOTH

Dandelions are named for lions, but not because of their golden, mane-like blooms. The French called the plant *dent-de-lion*, meaning "lion's tooth." That's because the leaves have jagged edges that slightly resemble sharp teeth.

WILDFLOWERS

LARGE-FLOWERED TRILLIUM
(TRILLIUM GRANDIFLORUM)

Large-flowered trilliums are woodland-loving wildflowers. They have the largest blooms in the trillium family. Each plant has three broad leaves and produces a single flower. The flower has three wavy-edged petals that start off white but slowly turn pale pink as the flower ages. In the fall, each plant produces a single red berry.

HOW TO SPOT

Height: 8 to 18 inches (20 to 46 cm)
Stem: Herbaceous
Leaves: Three broad, pointed leaves; 3 to 6 inches (7.6 to 15 cm) long
Flowers: White flowers with three triangle-shaped petals; 2 to 4 inches (5 to 10 cm) long
Range: North America
Habitat: Moist, deciduous forests
Bloom Period: Spring

FUN FACT
The large-flowered trillium is also known as the wood lily.

OXEYE DAISY
(LEUCANTHEMUM VULGARE)

Also called the common daisy, the oxeye daisy originated in Europe. Bright-white petals radiate from yellow centers. The daisy's stem holds leaves that get smaller the closer they are to the flower. Because they grow so quickly and overtake other plants, some places in the world see oxeye daises as harmful weeds.

HOW TO SPOT

Height: 1 to 3 feet (0.3 to 0.9 m)
Stem: Herbaceous
Leaves: Lobed, narrow leaves; up to 5 inches (12.7 cm) long
Flowers: White, disk-shaped flowers with yellow centers; up to 2 inches (5 cm) wide
Range: Asia, Australia, Europe, and North America
Habitat: Fields, pastures, and roadsides
Bloom Period: Summer

DAY'S EYES TO DAISY
The daisy was originally called day's eye. That's because of the way the flower opens in the morning and closes in the evening.

WILDFLOWERS

PASQUEFLOWER *(PULSATILLA PATENS)*

The pasqueflower is an early spring wildflower. It lives in the northern parts of the northern hemisphere, sometimes blooming while there's still snow on the ground. The pasqueflower has fern-like leaves. The entire plant—even the bell-shaped flower—is covered in a layer of soft, silky hair. The flowers can be pale lavender, purple, or blue.

HOW TO SPOT

Height: 8 to 12 inches (20 to 30 cm)
Stem: Herbaceous
Leaves: Lobed, basal leaves with long stalks
Flowers: Bell-shaped flowers; 1.5 to 2 inches (3.8 to 5 cm) wide
Range: Europe, North America, and northern Russia
Habitat: Prairies, meadows, and mountain slopes
Bloom Period: Spring and summer

FUN FACT
In old French, *pasque* refers to Easter. That's why this plant is called pasqueflower—it blooms in early spring, right around the Easter holiday.

PURPLE CONEFLOWER
(ECHINACEA PURPUREA)

The purple coneflower is a common wildflower in North America. Because of its adaptability to various growing conditions, it thrives in meadows, fields, and ditches. It can also be planted in gardens. Its narrow petals radiate from an orange center and drop downward. Its leaves and stem are covered in fine, stiff hairs. This gives the plant a rough texture.

HOW TO SPOT

Height: 2 to 5 feet (0.6 to 1.5 m)

Stem: Herbaceous

Leaves: Toothed, three-veined leaves; up to 8 inches (20 cm) long

Flowers: Disk-shaped flowers with orange centers; 3 to 6 inches (7.6 to 15 cm) wide

Range: North America

Habitat: Dry, sunny meadows, fields, or ditches

Bloom Period: Summer to mid-fall

WILDFLOWERS

QUEEN ANNE'S LACE
(DAUCUS CAROTA)

Queen Anne's lace is a tall meadow flower. These plants develop many umbrella-shaped clusters of tiny, white flowers. In the fall, the dried flower clusters curl up and resemble small birds' nests. Queen Anne's lace is considered an invasive weed throughout most of its range. The fast-spreading plant crowds out native plant species.

HOW TO SPOT

Height: 2 to 4 feet (0.6 to 1.2 m)
Stem: Herbaceous
Leaves: Thin, fern-like leaves; 5 inches (12.7 cm) long
Flowers: Umbrella-shaped clusters of tiny, white flowers; 3 to 6 inches (7.6 to 15 cm) wide
Range: Southwest Asia, Australia, Europe, and North America
Habitat: Fields and roadsides
Bloom Period: Summer and fall

RED COLUMBINE
(AQUILEGIA CANADENSIS)

The red columbine is a delicate-looking wildflower. It grows best in part shade to full sun, which is why it is often found in forests. Red columbines have three-lobed compound leaves. They also have red-and-yellow, bell-shaped flowers that hang down from thin stems.

FUN FACT
The red columbine's shape makes it difficult for most pollinators to reach its nectar. But hummingbirds and long-tongued moths have ideal mouthparts to reach into these flowers.

HOW TO SPOT
Height: 1 to 3 feet (0.3 to 0.9 m)
Stem: Herbaceous
Leaves: Three-lobed compound leaves; 1 to 3 inches (2.5 to 7.6 cm) long
Flowers: Red-and-yellow, bell-shaped flowers with pointed tips; 1 to 2 inches (2.5 to 5 cm) long
Range: North America
Habitat: Forests, hillsides, and roadsides
Bloom Period: Summer

WILDFLOWERS

STARFLOWER *(TRIENTALIS BOREALIS)*

Starflowers have white, star-shaped blooms that can have between five and nine pointed petals radiating from the centers. These flowers grow in moist environments, such as forests, and they're often found alongside mosses. Starflowers' leaves are large, pointed ovals that are usually a glossy green.

FUN FACT
Starflowers attract flies and bees. These insects feed on and collect pollen. Starflowers also attract chipmunks, who consume the plants' seeds.

HOW TO SPOT

Height: 4 to 8 inches (10 to 20 cm)
Stem: Herbaceous
Leaves: Pointed, oval leaves; 4 inches (10 cm) long
Flowers: White, star-shaped flowers with five to nine petals; 0.5 inches (1.3 cm) wide
Range: North America
Habitat: Conifer and deciduous forests
Bloom Period: Spring and summer

WHITE CLOVER *(TRIFOLIUM REPENS)*

The white clover is native to Europe. Today, these flowers are found throughout North America, where they are a common sight in lawns. White clovers are low, creeping plants with many compound leaves that have three leaflets. Each leaflet is green with two lighter green stripes. White clovers also produce small clusters of white flowers that can have pink edges.

HOW TO SPOT

Height: 4 inches (10 cm)
Stem: Herbaceous
Leaves: Compound leaves with three round leaflets; 1.5 inches (3.8 cm) wide
Flowers: Small, round clusters of white-and-pink flowers; 0.5 inches (1.3 cm) wide
Range: Asia, Europe, and North America
Habitat: Fields and lawns
Bloom Period: Spring and summer

FOUR-LEAF CLOVERS

White clovers' leaflets usually have only three leaves. However, these plants sometimes produce leaflets with four leaves that are known as lucky four-leaf clovers.

WILDFLOWERS

WILD LEEK *(ALLIUM TRICOCCUM)*

Wild leeks are spring wildflowers found in North American forests. They have long, green leaves that are reddish at the bases and produce small clusters of greenish-white flowers. Wild leeks are edible. They're part of the onion family. Their leaves and flowers have an onion scent, and the leaves and white bulbs can be used in recipes that call for onions.

HOW TO SPOT

Height: Up to 9 inches (23 cm)
Stem: Herbaceous
Leaves: Two to three long, narrow leaves; 6 to 12 inches (15 to 30 cm) long
Flowers: Small clusters of greenish-white flowers; 0.25 inches (0.64 cm) long
Range: North America
Habitat: Shady, moist forests
Bloom Period: Summer

FUN FACT
Wild leeks have several common names, including ramps, ramsons, and spring onions.

YELLOW GENTIAN *(GENTIANA ALBA)*

The yellow gentian is one of many species of gentians, a plant family known for its trumpet-shaped flowers. This species is native to North American prairies, but it is also grown in gardens. Yellow gentians have flowers that grow in clusters, and they can be white or white with a yellow or green tint. Like other species in the gentian family, yellow gentian flowers are tube-shaped. But unlike other gentians, yellow gentian flowers are closed at the ends rather than open like trumpets.

HOW TO SPOT

Height: 1 to 3 feet (0.3 to 0.9 m)

Stem: Herbaceous

Leaves: Smooth, pointed leaves; 5 inches (12.7 cm) long

Flowers: Round clusters of flowers that are closed at the ends; 1.5 to 2 inches (3.8 to 5 cm) long

Range: Central North America

Habitat: Prairies and fields

Bloom Period: Fall

GARDEN FLOWERS AND HERBS

COMMON LILAC *(SYRINGA VULGARIS)*

Common lilacs are native to Europe but are now grown in other places for their fragrant spring flowers. Lilacs have many small stems. They also have green, heart-shaped leaves and produce cone-shaped clusters of tiny, purple flowers in the spring. Other lilac species can have pink or white flowers.

FUN FACT
All lilac species are members of the olive family.

HOW TO SPOT

Height: 8 to 15 feet (2.4 to 4.6 m)
Stem: Woody
Leaves: Heart-shaped leaves; 3 to 6 inches (7.6 to 15 cm) long
Flowers: Cone-shaped clusters of tiny, purple flowers; up to 8 inches (20 cm) long
Range: Europe and North America
Habitat: Open woodlands, rocky hillsides, and gardens
Bloom Period: Spring

COMMON PEONY
(PAEONIA OFFICINALIS)

Peonies are flowering shrubs. They are known for their large, showy flowers that bloom in the spring. The common peony is one of 30 peony species. These flowers have bright-green leaves and produce large, red-pink flowers that have yellow centers. Like most peonies, the flowers of common peonies have strong, sweet fragrances. Peony flowers often attract ants, but these insects don't harm the plants.

HOW TO SPOT

Height: 1.5 to 3 feet (0.45 to 0.9 m)
Stem: Herbaceous
Leaves: Divided, compound leaves
Flowers: Cup-shaped flowers with yellow centers; up to 5 inches (12.7 cm) wide
Range: Europe and North America
Habitat: Open woodlands and gardens
Bloom Period: Spring

GARDEN FLOWERS AND HERBS

COMMON SUNFLOWER
(HELIANTHUS ANNUUS)

Many of the large sunflowers grown in gardens are cultivars of the common sunflower. Common sunflowers have tall, upright stems. They also have large, sandpaper-like leaves and multiple branching stems at the tops. Each plant produces several large, yellow flowers that bloom in the summer and produce many edible seeds in the fall.

FUN FACT
Sunflowers got their name because their blooms follow the sun's path as it crosses the sky.

HOW TO SPOT

Height: 3 to 10 feet (0.9 to 3 m)
Stem: Herbaceous
Leaves: Triangular or heart-shaped leaves with coarse-toothed edges; up to 12 inches (30 cm) long
Flowers: Saucer-shaped flowers with yellow petals surrounding dark-brown centers; 3 to 6 inches (7.6 to 15 cm) wide
Range: North America
Habitat: Moist forests, fields, roadsides, and gardens
Bloom Period: Summer and fall

DILL *(ANETHUM GRAVEOLENS)*

Dill is a perennial herb grown for its appearance and for cooking purposes. Its stem sprouts branches of lacy, fern-like leaves and umbrella-shaped flower clusters. In the fall, dill seeds can be harvested and used in cooking.

HOW TO SPOT

Height: 2 to 3 feet (0.6 to 0.9 m)
Stem: Herbaceous
Leaves: Fern-like leaves
Flowers: Umbrella-like clusters of yellow flowers; 1 to 3.5 inches (2.5 to 9 cm) wide
Range: Asia, Europe, and North America
Habitat: Gardens
Bloom Period: Summer and fall

GARDEN FLOWERS AND HERBS

ENGLISH LAVENDER
(LAVANDULA ANGUSTIFOLIA)

English lavender is not actually from England. It's a perennial herb from the Mediterranean region. English lavender grows in clumps of dense, straight stems that have tiny, gray-green leaves. In the summer, lavender has many spike-like clusters of small, purple flowers.

HOW TO SPOT

Height: 2 to 3 feet (0.6 to 0.9 m)
Stem: Semiwoody
Leaves: Narrow, gray-green leaves; up to 2.5 inches (6.3 cm) long
Flowers: Spike-like clusters of purple flowers; 0.7 to 3 inches (1.7 to 7.6 cm) long
Range: Europe and North America
Habitat: Dry, sunny fields and gardens
Bloom Period: Late spring to summer

FUN FACT
Lavender leaves and flowers are used in cooking. These plants also have oils that people use to create essential oils and perfumes.

FRENCH MARIGOLD
(TAGETES PATULA)

The French marigold is one of about 50 marigold species. It comes from Mexico and Guatemala. It became popular in France in the 1500s. French marigolds are bushy, low-growing annuals that have fern-like compound leaves and bright, compact flowers. The flowers are saucer-shaped. They can be shades of orange, red, yellow, or a combination of these colors.

HOW TO SPOT

Height: 6 to 12 inches (15 to 30 cm)
Stem: Herbaceous
Leaves: Compound leaves of toothed leaflets; up to 6 inches (15 cm) long
Flowers: Small, saucer-shaped flowers with layers of petals; 1 to 2 inches (2.5 to 5 cm) wide
Range: Native to Mexico and Guatemala
Habitat: Gardens
Bloom Period: Spring and fall

GARDEN FLOWERS AND HERBS

HYBRID TEA ROSE *(ROSA)*

The *Rosa* genus has more than 100 species of roses and thousands of cultivars. The most popular roses among gardeners today are hybrid tea roses. These roses have thorny stems and compound leaves. They produce a single rose per stem. The flowers can be a variety of colors, depending on the specific cultivar.

FUN FACT

All of today's hybrid tea rose cultivars can be traced back to one rose called La France that was developed in 1867. The botanical names for hybrid tea roses are created by using *Rosa* followed by their cultivar name. For example, the flower developed in 1867 is called *Rosa* "La France."

HOW TO SPOT

Height: 3 to 8 feet (0.9 to 2.4 m)
Stem: Herbaceous
Leaves: Compound leaves
Flowers: Cup-shaped blooms; up to 7 inches (18 cm) wide
Range: Worldwide, usually in temperate climates
Habitat: Gardens
Bloom Period: Summer

IMPATIENS *(IMPATIENS WALLERIANA)*

Impatiens are flowers that thrive in cool shade. They first grew in African rain forests. Today, they're one of the most popular garden plants in the United States. Impatiens have thick succulent stems. They grow into large mounds of dense leaves and colorful flowers that bloom all summer. Depending on the cultivar, impatiens can be a variety of colors, including shades of pink, red, orange, purple, and white.

HOW TO SPOT

Height: 6 to 24 inches (15 to 61 cm)
Stem: Herbaceous
Leaves: Pointed, oval leaves; up to 3 inches (7.6 cm) long
Flowers: Five-petaled flowers; 1 to 3 inches (2.5 to 7.6 cm) wide
Range: Native to Africa
Habitat: Shady gardens and containers
Bloom Period: Summer and fall

GARDEN FLOWERS AND HERBS

LILY OF THE VALLEY
(CONVALLARIA MAJALIS)

The lily of the valley grows in forests and is commonly planted in gardens throughout the world. In the spring, each plant sprouts two to three long leaves and an arching stem that has several white, bell-shaped flowers. The flowers have a strong, sweet scent, but the plant is poisonous if eaten.

HOW TO SPOT

Height: 6 to 12 inches (15 to 30 cm)
Stem: Herbaceous
Leaves: Two to three large, pointed, oval leaves; 5 to 10 inches (12.7 to 25 cm) long
Flowers: Arching stem of five to ten white, bell-shaped flowers; flowers are less than 1 inch (2.5 cm) long
Range: Worldwide
Habitat: Forests and gardens
Bloom Period: Spring

SPEARMINT *(MENTHA SPICATA)*

There are many plant species in the mint family, including those that grow in the wild, but spearmint is the most popular mint grown in gardens. This perennial herb spreads quickly. Its flexible stem is full of small, fragrant leaves. People can eat the leaves fresh, or they can dry the leaves and use them in cooking. In the summer, spearmints produce clusters of tiny flowers.

HOW TO SPOT

Height: 1 to 2 feet (0.3 to 0.6 m)
Stem: Herbaceous
Leaves: Pointed, oval leaves with toothed edges; 1 to 3 inches (2.5 to 7.6 cm) long
Flowers: Dense spikes of small, pinkish-white flowers; 1 to 6 inches (2.5 to 15 cm) long
Range: Europe and North America
Habitat: Gardens and moist forests
Bloom Period: Summer

FUN FACT
Spearmint leaves are used to flavor teas, candies, sauces, beverages, and syrups.

VINES

BOUGAINVILLEA
(BOUGAINVILLEA GLABRA)

The bougainvillea, sometimes called the lesser bougainvillea, is a flowering vine from South America. Lesser bougainvilleas have woody vines, green leaves, and tiny, tube-shaped flowers. The flowers are surrounded by colorful bracts (or specialized leaves) that, depending on the species, can be yellow, pink, purple, red, or white. These bracts are often mistaken for flower petals.

HOW TO SPOT

Height: 10 to 20 feet (3 to 6 m)
Stem: Woody
Leaves: Pointed, oval leaves; 3 to 6 inches (7.6 to 15 cm) long
Flowers: Clusters of tiny, tube-shaped flowers surrounded by colorful bracts
Range: South America
Habitat: Gardens and subtropical and tropical woods
Bloom Period: Spring and summer

EUROPEAN IVY *(HEDERA HELIX)*

European ivy is a fast-growing perennial vine that's native to Europe and Asia. This shrub-like plant either spreads along the ground or climbs trees and structures such as walls and buildings. European ivies have flexible stems covered with three- to five-lobed green leaves. In some places, this ivy is considered an invasive species in the wild. It can harm native plants and habitats.

FUN FACT
European ivy is also known as common ivy. It has long been a popular houseplant.

HOW TO SPOT

Height: 20 to 80 feet (6 to 24 m)
Stem: Woody
Leaves: Pointed leaves with three to five lobes; 4 inches (10 cm) long
Flowers: Umbrella-shaped clusters of small, greenish-white flowers; flowers are less than 1 inch (2.5 cm) long
Range: Native to Europe and Asia
Habitat: Deciduous forests, urban forests, and shrublands
Bloom Period: Summer and fall

VINES

GRAPE HONEYSUCKLE
(LONICERA RETICULATA)

Grape honeysuckle is a woody vine. It belongs to the honeysuckle family, a group of plants that has 180 species of shrubs and vines. Grape honeysuckle is native to North America and usually grows in moist forests and thickets. If there isn't a tree or structure nearby to climb, the plant will sometimes appear as a leafy mound or shrub. Grape honeysuckles have rounded green leaves. In the summer, these plants have clusters of yellow, tube-shaped flowers.

HOW TO SPOT

Height: 10 to 15 feet (3 to 4.6 m)
Stem: Woody
Leaves: Rounded leaves; 1.5 to 3.5 inches (3.8 to 9 cm) long
Flowers: Clusters of yellow, tube-shaped flowers with long stamens; up to 1 inch (2.5 cm) long
Fruits: Round, red berries; up to 0.5 inches (1.3 cm) long
Range: North America
Habitat: Moist forests and riverbanks
Bloom Period: Spring and summer

JAPANESE WISTERIA
(WISTERIA FLORIBUNDA)

The Japanese wisteria is known for its fragrance and abundant flowers. This climbing vine is native to Japan. People brought it to other countries as a garden plant. Today, it is often grown on fences, trellises, and buildings. In the spring, it has large, drooping clusters of pinkish-purple flowers. In some parts of the world, wisteria species are aggressive, invasive plants that crowd out native plants in the wild.

HOW TO SPOT

Height: 10 to 25 feet (3 to 7.6 m)
Stem: Woody
Leaves: Compound leaves with 15 to 19 leaflets; 1 to 1.3 feet (0.3 to 0.4 m) long
Flowers: Drooping clusters of pinkish-purple flowers; 1 to 1.5 feet (0.3 to 0.45 m) long
Range: Asia, Europe, and North America
Habitat: Forests and gardens
Bloom Period: Spring

FUN FACT
Bark from the Japanese wisteria can be used to make rope.

VINES

MORNING GLORY
(IPOMOEA PURPUREA)

Morning glory is a popular garden plant that's often grown on a trellis or wall. It's a fast-growing, climbing vine. These plants have green, heart-shaped leaves. They also have purple, trumpet-shaped flowers that open in the morning and close in the afternoon. That's why the plant's common name is morning glory.

HOW TO SPOT

Height: 6 to 10 feet (1.8 to 3 m)
Stem: Herbaceous
Leaves: Heart-shaped leaves; up to 4 inches (10 cm) long
Flowers: Purple, trumpet-shaped flowers; up to 2.5 inches (6.3 cm) wide
Range: North America, Central America, and South America
Habitat: Open forests and gardens
Bloom Period: Summer and fall

PASSION FRUIT *(PASSIFLORA EDULIS)*

Passion fruit is a climbing vine that's native to South America. It's now grown in tropical and subtropical locations around the world. Passion fruits are known for both their showy flowers and their fruits. Their large, bowl-shaped flowers have purple centers and white edges. The plant produces a deep-purple, rounded fruit known as passion fruit.

FUN FACT
Passion fruit can be eaten raw or used to make food products such as beverages, jellies, and sherbets.

HOW TO SPOT

Height: 10 to 15 feet (3 to 4.6 m)
Stem: Woody
Leaves: Three-lobed leaves with toothed edges; 3 to 8 inches (7.6 to 20 cm) long
Flowers: Bowl-shaped, purple-and-white flowers; up to 3 inches (7.6 cm) wide
Fruits: Oval-shaped, purple fruits; up to 2 inches (5 cm) wide
Range: Worldwide
Habitat: Tropical and subtropical areas
Bloom Period: Seasonal

VINES

STAR JASMINE
(TRACHELOSPERMUM JASMINOIDES)

Star jasmine is a perennial vine with fragrant, star-shaped, white flowers that bloom in the spring. It can appear as a shrub, a ground cover, or a climbing vine. Depending on its location and environment, the star jasmine's glossy, green leaves may turn red or drop off the plant in the fall.

HOW TO SPOT

Height: 3 to 6 feet (0.9 to 1.8 m)
Stem: Woody
Leaves: Oval leaves; 3.5 inches (9 cm) long
Flowers: Clusters of white, star-shaped flowers; up to 1 inch (2.5 cm) wide
Range: Asia, Europe, and North America
Habitat: Sunny gardens or containers
Bloom Period: Spring

VIRGINIA CREEPER
(PARTHENOCISSUS QUINQUEFOLIA)

As its name suggests, the Virginia creeper is a plant known for either creeping along the ground or climbing structures. Virginia creepers have small, sucker-like discs that grow along the vines and help them attach to trees and other surfaces. In the spring, Virginia creepers produce clusters of white flowers. In the fall, their green compound leaves turn shades of purple and red.

HOW TO SPOT

Height: Up to 90 feet (27 m)

Stem: Woody

Leaves: Compound leaves with four to five leaflets; up to 6 inches (15 cm) long

Flowers: Branching clusters of white flowers; 3 to 6 inches (7.6 to 15 cm) long

Range: North America

Habitat: Deciduous forests and bluffs

Bloom Period: Summer

FUN FACT

People sometimes grow Virginia creepers outside their homes. However, if allowed to run wild, these vines can damage window shutters, gutters, and even electrical wiring.

BERRIES AND SHRUBS

AMERICAN CRANBERRY
(VACCINIUM MACROCARPON)

The American cranberry is native to North America. Cranberries are grown for their tart fruits that can be made into juices, sauces, and other products. American cranberries grow as either vines or small shrubs, and they have small, glossy leaves. In the fall, their pink-and-white flowers become oval-shaped, red fruits called cranberries.

HOW TO SPOT

Height: 9 to 12 inches (23 to 30 cm)
Stem: Woody
Leaves: Oval leaves; less than 1 inch (2.5 cm) long
Flowers: Clusters of drooping pink-and-white flowers; less than 1 inch (2.5 cm) long
Range: North America
Habitat: Bogs, swamps, and shorelines
Bloom Period: Spring and summer

BLACK RASPBERRY
(RUBUS OCCIDENTALIS)

Black raspberry plants are known for their small, edible fruits and thorny stems. These plants have compound leaves with three to five leaflets per leaf. The leaflets also have toothed edges and fuzzy undersides. In the spring, black raspberry plants produce white flowers that eventually turn into fruits. The fruits start out red, then turn a very dark purple—nearly black—when they're ripe.

HOW TO SPOT

Height: 3 to 5 feet (0.9 to 1.5 m)

Stem: Woody

Leaves: Compound leaves with three to five leaflets; 2 to 4 inches (5 to 10 cm) long

Flowers: White flowers with five petals; up to 0.5 inches (1.3 cm) wide

Fruits: Dark-purple raspberries; 0.5 inches (1.3 cm) long

Range: North America

Habitat: Deciduous forests, roadsides, and disturbed areas

Bloom Period: Spring

BERRIES AND SHRUBS

BOXWOOD *(BUXUS SEMPERVIRENS)*

Boxwoods are dense evergreen shrubs that keep their small, glossy, green leaves year-round. Boxwoods have many short branches, but under certain conditions they can also look like small trees. In the spring, boxwoods produce clusters of small, yellowish-green flowers.

FUN FACT
Boxwoods are often used as hedges. People may also make topiaries or wreaths out of them. Topiaries are plants that people have shaped into art.

HOW TO SPOT
Height: 5 to 15 feet (1.5 to 4.6 m)
Stem: Woody
Leaves: Small, oval leaves; 0.5 to 1.5 inches (1.3 to 3.8 cm) long
Flowers: Small clusters of greenish-yellow flowers; flowers are less than 1 inch (2.5 cm) long
Range: Africa, Asia, Europe, and North America
Habitat: Open forests and rocky hillsides
Bloom Period: Spring

BUNCHBERRY *(CORNUS CANADENSIS)*

The bunchberry is a very small deciduous shrub. It thrives in shady forests in northern climates. It grows low to the ground and is known for its ability to spread quickly. Bunchberries have glossy, green leaves. Their flowers bloom in tiny clusters. Each cluster is surrounded by four white bracts that look like flower petals. In the fall, bunchberries have clusters of small, red berries.

HOW TO SPOT

Height: Up to 9 inches (23 cm)
Stem: Woody
Leaves: Pointed, oval leaves in clusters of four to six leaves; 1 to 2 inches (2.5 to 5 cm) long
Flowers: Clusters of tiny flowers surrounded by four white bracts; up to 1 inch (2.5 cm) wide
Fruits: Round, red berries; 0.25 inches (0.64 cm) wide
Range: Asia, Greenland, and North America
Habitat: Forests
Bloom Period: Early summer

BERRIES AND SHRUBS

CACAO TREE *(THEOBROMA CACAO)*

The cacao tree is also called the cocoa tree, and it's best known for being the source of chocolate. These plants have spindly branches and large, oval leaves that are green year-round. Cacao trees have clusters of tiny flowers that eventually grow into large, egg-shaped fruits called cocoa pods. Each pod contains 30 to 40 seeds known as cocoa beans.

HOW TO SPOT

Height: Up to 26 feet (8 m)
Stem: Woody
Leaves: Large, oval leaves; 15 inches (38 cm) long
Flowers: Clusters of small, pink flowers
Fruits: Yellowish-orange, oval pods; 6 to 10 inches (15 to 25 cm) long
Range: North America, Central America, and South America
Habitat: Moist forests
Bloom Period: Year-round

COCOA BEANS

The seeds from cacao trees are the most important ingredient in chocolate. People cut through cocoa pods with sharp knives to reveal clusters of wet seeds inside. Then they scrape the seeds out and dry them. Dried seeds are used to make both cocoa butter and cocoa powder, which can then be made into chocolate.

CLOUDBERRY *(RUBUS CHAMAEMORUS)*

Cloudberry plants thrive in moist soils and cool temperatures. They are native to the Arctic, where they grow in bogs and on the tundra. These low-growing plants spread across the ground and have green, leathery leaves. In the summer, the white flowers turn into cloudberries, which are yellowish-orange fruits that look a bit like raspberries.

HOW TO SPOT

Height: 8 to 12 inches (20 to 30 cm)
Stem: Woody
Leaves: Simple leaves with three to seven rounded lobes; 1.5 to 4.25 inches (3.8 to 10.7 cm) long
Flowers: White flowers with four or five rounded petals; up to 1.25 inches (3 cm) wide
Fruits: Yellow-orange, raspberry-like fruits; up to 0.75 inches (1.9 cm) wide
Range: Arctic and subarctic regions
Habitat: Boreal forests, bogs, and tundra
Bloom Period: Summer

FUN FACT
Cloudberries are a circumpolar species. This means they are found in the regions around the North Pole.

BERRIES AND SHRUBS

ENGLISH HOLLY *(ILEX AQUIFOLIUM)*

English holly is an evergreen plant that can appear as a shrub or be used as a hedge in gardens or fields. The English holly's glossy leaves have sharp spines along their edges and stay green throughout the year. In the fall and winter, the plant produces tiny berries that are usually red but can also be orange or yellow.

HOW TO SPOT

Height: 30 to 50 feet (9 to 15 m)
Stem: Woody
Leaves: Glossy, sharp-edged leaves; 1 to 3 inches (2.5 to 7.6 cm) long
Flowers: Small, greenish-white flowers; less than 1 inch (2.5 cm) wide
Fruits: Small, red berries; 0.25 inches (0.64 cm) wide
Range: Africa, Asia, Europe, and North America
Habitat: Forests and gardens
Bloom Period: Spring

FUN FACT
English holly's evergreen leaves and red berries have made it a popular Christmas decoration.

EUROPEAN ELDER (SAMBUCUS NIGRA)

European elders are shrubs with many stems. During the growing seasons, European elders are recognized by their delicate, umbrella-shaped clusters of white flowers. Later, the flowers become clusters of round, black fruits called elderberries. People use both the flowers and berries in cooking.

HOW TO SPOT

Height: 8 to 20 feet (2.4 to 6 m)
Stem: Woody
Leaves: Compound leaves of three to seven leaflets; up to 5 inches (12.7 cm) long
Flowers: Umbrella-shaped clusters of tiny, white flowers; up to 10 inches (25 cm) wide
Fruits: Clusters of black elderberries; fruits are less than 1 inch (2.5 cm) long
Range: Africa, Asia, and Europe
Habitat: Open forests and gardens
Bloom Period: Summer

FUN FACT
The European elder's bark, leaves, and raw berries are poisonous.

BERRIES AND SHRUBS

JAPANESE CAMELLIA
(CAMELLIA JAPONICA)

The Japanese camellia is an evergreen shrub. It's native to Japan but has become popular worldwide as a garden plant. These plants have thick, glossy leaves that are dark green. They also have clusters of round flowers. The flowers are often pruned after they first appear so that a larger single flower grows in the place of each cluster. Like other camellia species, Japanese camellia flowers can be a range of colors, including white, pink, red, yellow, and lavender.

HOW TO SPOT

Height: 7 to 12 feet (2 to 3.6 m)
Stem: Woody
Leaves: Oval, leathery leaves; 3 to 4 inches (7.6 to 10 cm) long
Flowers: Clusters of round flowers with many petals; 3 to 5 inches (7.6 to 12.7 cm) wide
Range: Worldwide
Habitat: Gardens
Bloom Period: Spring or winter, depending on the climate

FUN FACT
People sometimes call the Japanese camellia the rose of winter.

LOWBUSH BLUEBERRY
(VACCINIUM ANGUSTIFOLIUM)

The lowbush blueberry is a low-growing deciduous shrub that is both wild and cultivated. These plants are common in the northern conifer forests of North America, where they are important food sources for black bears, deer, and moose. Lowbush blueberry plants have many woody stems and green leaves with finely toothed edges. In the spring, these plants grow clusters of bell-shaped flowers that later mature into blueberries.

HOW TO SPOT

Height: 12 to 20 inches (30 to 51 cm)
Stem: Woody
Leaves: Pointed, oval leaves with finely serrated edges; 0.75 to 1.5 inches (1.9 to 3.8 cm) long
Flowers: Clusters of small, white, bell-shaped flowers; 0.25 inches (0.64 cm) long
Fruits: Round blueberries; up to 0.3 inches (0.7 cm) wide
Range: Northern North America
Habitat: Open conifer woods and fields
Bloom Period: Summer

FUN FACT

Lowbush blueberries are small and sweet, so they're often used in making jams. Another species, highbush blueberries, are typically sold whole in stores.

BERRIES AND SHRUBS

SAND CHERRY *(PRUNUS PUMILA)*

The sand cherry is a deciduous shrub that produces large fruits. These fruits can be reddish-purple to almost black and have one hard seed inside. Sand cherries usually grow in sandy soils in prairies, savannas, or dunes. They have shiny green leaves and produce clusters of white flowers in the spring.

HOW TO SPOT

Height: 1 to 6 feet (0.3 to 1.8 m)
Stem: Woody
Leaves: Pointed, oval leaves; 1.5 to 2.5 inches (3.8 to 6.3 cm) long
Flowers: Clusters of white flowers with five petals; 0.5 inches (1.3 cm) wide
Fruits: Round, reddish-purple to black fruits; up to 0.5 inches (1.3 cm) wide
Range: North America
Habitat: Prairies, savannas, and dunes
Bloom Period: Summer

STAGHORN SUMAC *(RHUS TYPHINA)*

The staghorn sumac is the largest of all sumac species. Although it's technically a shrub, it can often look like a small tree. Staghorn sumacs have many branches coated with layers of fine hairs. This gives the branches a soft texture similar to the velvet on young deer antlers. Staghorn sumacs have large, green, compound leaves. In the fall, these leaves turn red. Staghorn sumacs produce many spike-shaped clusters of reddish-brown fruits.

HOW TO SPOT

Height: 15 to 25 feet (4.5 to 7.6 m)
Stem: Woody
Leaves: Compound leaves of nine to 27 leaflets; up to 1.5 feet (0.45 m) long
Flowers: Pointed clusters of tiny, greenish-yellow flowers; up to 8 inches (20 cm) long
Fruits: Pointed clusters of red, berry-like fruits; up to 8 inches (20 cm) long
Range: North America
Habitat: Forests, stream banks, and roadsides
Bloom Period: Summer

FUN FACT
Staghorn sumac fruits can be ground into powders and used as seasonings.

BERRIES AND SHRUBS

TEA PLANT *(CAMELLIA SINENSIS)*

The most widely grown camellia species in the world is the tea plant. These plants are slow-growing, dense evergreen shrubs with dark leaves and fragrant white flowers. Tea plants' leaves are harvested and dried to make tea, a drink that's consumed all over the world. The tea plant is also grown as a decorative plant or hedge.

HOW TO SPOT

Height: 6 to 15 feet (1.8 to 4.6 m)
Stem: Woody
Leaves: Oval-shaped leaves with serrated edges; 3 to 6 inches (7.6 to 15 cm) long
Flowers: White flowers; 1 to 3 inches (2.5 to 7.6 cm) wide
Range: Africa, Asia, and South America
Habitat: Cultivated fields and gardens
Bloom Period: Fall and winter

BLACK AND GREEN TEA

Black tea and green tea are both made from tea plant leaves. For green tea, the leaves are picked and then steamed to prevent them from losing their green color. This process also gives green tea a different flavor than black tea. To make black tea, the leaves are picked and rolled. Then they are exposed to air so they darken.

TRUE INDIGO *(INDIGOFERA TINCTORIA)*

True indigo is a tropical shrub. It was once widely used to create a dark-blue dye called indigo. The plant itself is not blue at all. It has compound leaves of several green leaflets. In the summer, these plants have clusters of pink or violet flowers. After blooming, true indigo produces seed pods that can be up to 2 inches (5 cm) long.

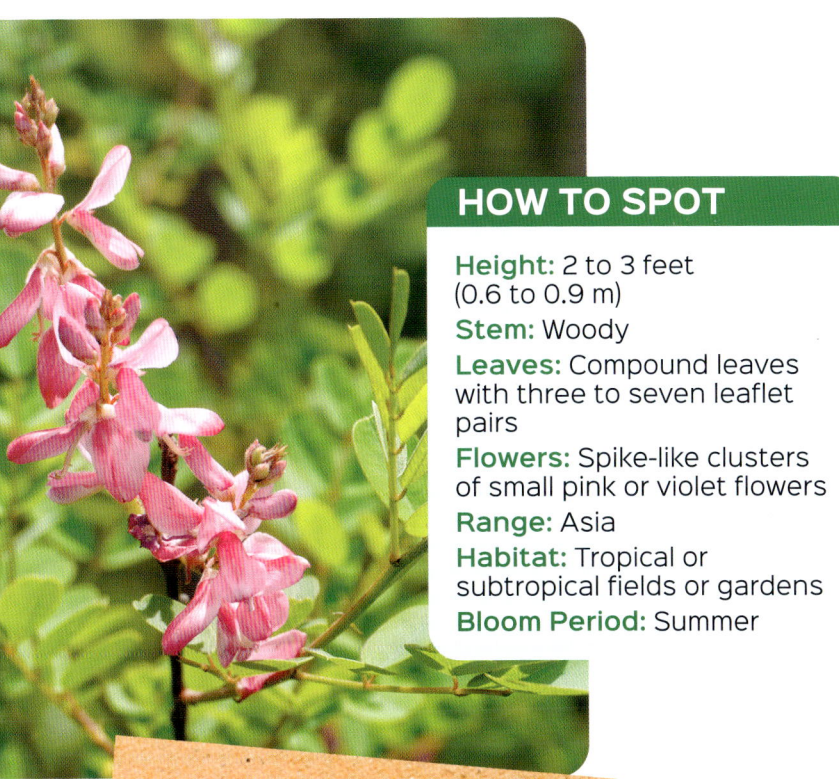

HOW TO SPOT

Height: 2 to 3 feet (0.6 to 0.9 m)
Stem: Woody
Leaves: Compound leaves with three to seven leaflet pairs
Flowers: Spike-like clusters of small pink or violet flowers
Range: Asia
Habitat: Tropical or subtropical fields or gardens
Bloom Period: Summer

FUN FACT
Making dye from the true indigo plant is a complicated process with several steps. Indigo leaves must undergo fermentation (a chemical change) in order to produce the dye's blue color. Most indigo-colored dye used today is not made from plants.

BERRIES AND SHRUBS

WILD BLACK CURRANT
(RIBES AMERICANUM)

There are more than 100 species of currants. This is a family of shrubs that produces round berries—called currants—that are used in jams, jellies, and flavorings. Wild black currants grow in cool, moist habitats in the northern parts of North America. Wild black currants have smooth, thornless stems and coarse, lobed leaves. Currants grow in clusters. The fruits turn black when ripe.

HOW TO SPOT

Height: 2 to 5 feet (0.6 to 1.5 m)
Stem: Woody
Leaves: Wide leaves with three to five lobes and toothed edges; 1 to 2 inches (2.5 to 5 cm) long
Flowers: Dangling clusters of six to 20 pale-yellow, bell-shaped flowers; flowers are 0.5 inches (1.3 cm) long
Fruits: Smooth, round, black berries; up to 0.3 inches (0.8 cm) wide
Range: North America
Habitat: Open forests, swamps, and stream banks
Bloom Period: Spring and summer

WILD STRAWBERRY
(FRAGARIA VESCA)

The wild strawberry is one of many strawberry species, and it can be found growing in the wild or in gardens. Wild strawberries have horizontal stems that help these plants spread along the ground. Wild strawberries are everbearing, which means they continue to produce flowers and fruits throughout the growing season and will often have fruits and flowers on them at the same time.

HOW TO SPOT

Height: 4 to 8 inches (10 to 20 cm)
Stem: Herbaceous
Leaves: Compound leaves with three toothed leaflets; up to 1 inch (2.5 cm) long
Flowers: Small, white flowers with five petals and yellow centers; 0.5 inches (1.3 cm) wide
Fruits: Bright-red strawberries; 0.5 inches (1.3 cm) long
Range: Asia, Europe, and North America
Habitat: Open forests and gardens
Bloom Period: Spring and summer

FUN FACT
Since wild strawberries are bright red and small, they're often grown in gardens or containers for decoration rather than for eating.

CARNIVOROUS PLANTS

COMMON BLADDERWORT
(UTRICULARIA VULGARIS)

Common bladderworts don't have any roots. Instead, these carnivorous plants float on the water's surface in freshwater habitats, such as lakes, ponds, and wetlands. Common bladderworts have many stems and needle-like leaves. These plants have small sacs called bladders that are used to catch tiny, aquatic organisms for food.

HOW TO SPOT

Height: 1 to 3 feet (0.3 to 0.9 m)
Stem: Herbaceous
Leaves: Many needle-like leaves along multibranched stems; 0.75 to 2 inches (1.9 to 5 cm) long
Flowers: Small clusters of yellow flowers; 0.5 to 0.75 inches (1.3 to 1.9 cm) wide
Range: Throughout the northern hemisphere
Habitat: Lakes, wetlands, ponds, and streams
Bloom Period: Summer

FUN FACT
The tiny sacs on common bladderworts have hairs. When small organisms brush against these hairs, the sacs spring open and suck in the organisms.

COMMON SUNDEW
(DROSERA ROTUNDIFOLIA)

There are more than 150 species of sundews, and each of them is carnivorous. The term *sundew* comes from the drops of nectar the plants use to attract insects. Sundew plants look like they're covered with dew. Low-growing common sundews have round, paddle-shaped leaves that are covered with red hairs. Insects get stuck when they land on the sticky substance that coats the common sundews' leaves.

HOW TO SPOT

Height: 2 to 10 inches (5 to 25 cm)

Stem: Herbaceous

Leaves: Round, sticky leaves with red hairs; 0.75 inches (1.9 cm) wide

Flowers: Small clusters of white flowers on long, leafless stems; 0.25 inches (0.64 cm) wide

Range: Asia, Europe, and North America

Habitat: Bogs and wetlands

Bloom Period: Summer

CARNIVOROUS PLANTS

Most plants get their nutrients through the soil and photosynthesis. Carnivorous plants get some or all of their nutrients from consuming animals, such as insects or even frogs. These plants tend to attract prey with nectar. Then they trap the prey with a sticky or slippery substance that makes it impossible for the prey to escape. Some plants, like Venus flytraps, can close on prey, trapping them inside.

CARNIVOROUS PLANTS

VENUS FLYTRAP *(DIONAEA MUSCIPULA)*

Venus flytraps are endangered carnivorous plants that get most of their necessary nutrients from consuming insects. At the end of each leaf, the Venus flytrap has a clam-shaped growth with spines along the edges and trigger hairs inside. If an insect lands on the plant and touches two trigger hairs, the trap quickly closes. The plant then produces enzymes that break down and digest the insect.

FUN FACT
Carnivorous plants such as the Venus flytrap might look dangerous, but they can't actually harm humans.

HOW TO SPOT

Height: 6 to 12 inches (15 to 30 cm)
Stem: Herbaceous
Leaves: Rosettes of up to eight blade-shaped leaves with hinged traps on the ends; 2 to 5 inches (5 to 12.7 cm) long
Flowers: Cluster of white, cup-shaped flowers on long stems; less than 1 inch (2.5 cm) long
Range: North America
Habitat: Marshes, wet grasslands, and savannas
Bloom Period: Summer

YELLOW PITCHER PLANT
(SARRACENIA FLAVA)

Yellow pitcher plants lure in nearby insects with nectar. Then the plants trap the insects. These plants have yellowish-green leaves that grow straight from the ground and look like trumpets. These are called pitchers. The insides of the pitchers are coated with slippery, ultrafine hairs. Once insects are inside, they can't escape.

HOW TO SPOT

Height: 1.5 to 3 feet (0.45 to 0.9 m)
Stem: None
Leaves: Tall, yellowish-green, trumpet-shaped leaves with horizontal lids; 1.6 to 3 feet (0.48 to 0.9 m) tall
Flowers: Yellow flowers with five petals; up to 2 inches (5 cm) wide
Range: North America
Habitat: Sandy bogs and savannas
Bloom Period: Spring

FERNS

BIRD'S-NEST FERN *(ASPLENIUM NIDUS)*

Bird's-nest ferns are tropical evergreen plants with large, leathery leaves. The leaves grow in rosette arrangements and can be up to 5 feet (1.5 m) long. When inner fronds die, they turn brown and curl up into the center of the plant, resembling a bird's nest.

HOW TO SPOT

Height: 3 to 5 feet (0.9 to 1.5 m)
Stem: Herbaceous
Leaves: Smooth, wavy-edged leaves that grow in rosettes; 4 to 5 feet (1.2 to 1.5 m) long
Range: Southeast Asia, Australia, Hawaii, Madagascar, North America, and Polynesia
Habitat: Rain forests and gardens

WHAT ARE FERNS?

Ferns are plants that don't have flowers or seeds. Instead, they reproduce through cells called spores. Before they are released, spores are contained in capsules. These usually appear as tiny bumps on the undersides of ferns' leaves.

LADY FERN *(ATHYRIUM FILIX-FEMINA)*

Lady ferns are green plants with tall, lacy leaves called fronds that sprout from the ground, usually in upright clumps. The undersides of the leaves are covered in tiny dots called spores that lady ferns use to reproduce. Lady ferns are perennial, so their leaves drop in the fall. New ones grow in the spring.

HOW TO SPOT

Height: 2 to 5 feet (0.6 to 1.5 m)
Stem: Herbaceous
Leaves: Lacy fronds; up to 1 foot (0.3 m) wide and 3 feet (0.9 m) long
Range: North America
Habitat: Moist forests, meadows, and swamps

FUN FACT
Many fern species do well in low light, which is one of the reasons they're popular houseplants.

FERNS

OSTRICH FERN
(MATTEUCCIA STRUTHIOPTERIS)

With their long, feather-like fronds, it's easy to see how ostrich ferns got their name. In the spring, ostrich ferns first appear as small, curled sprouts. They gradually grow and uncurl into large, green fronds. In midsummer, the ostrich fern produces at least one woody, dark-brown frond in its center. This frond contains the spores that allow the fern to reproduce.

HOW TO SPOT

Height: 3 to 6 feet (0.9 to 1.8 m)
Stem: Herbaceous
Leaves: Feather-like fronds; up to 4 feet (1.2 m) long
Range: Eastern Asia, Europe, and North America
Habitat: Moist, shady forests

FUN FACT
The ostrich fern's first sprouts are called fiddleheads. These are edible, but they must be washed and cooked very carefully in order to be eaten safely.

ROYAL FERN *(OSMUNDA REGALIS)*

Since royal ferns have double compound leaves instead of feathery fronds, it's easy to mistake them for shrubs rather than ferns. Royal ferns have spores that look like flower clusters. These grow on tassel-like stalks. Like other fern species, royal ferns thrive in cool, moist environments and are often found in shaded areas near water.

HOW TO SPOT

Height: 2 to 3 feet (0.6 to 0.9 m)

Stem: Herbaceous

Leaves: Double compound leaves of several leaflets; up to 3 feet (0.9 m) long

Range: North America

Habitat: Swamps, wet forests, stream banks, and bluffs

MOSSES

BONFIRE MOSS
(FUNARIA HYGROMETRICA)

Bonfire moss can grow in many places with moist soil, but it's commonly found in areas that have been recently burned. Like all mosses, the stems and leaves of bonfire mosses are very small. Up close, the leaves look like tiny, green threads with beads on the ends. Those beads are spore capsules, which bonfire mosses use to reproduce.

HOW TO SPOT

Height: 0.15 to 0.4 inches (0.38 to 1 cm)
Stem: Herbaceous
Leaves: Thread-like leaves with spore capsules on the ends; 0.07 to 0.1 inches (0.17 to 0.25 cm) long
Range: Asia, Australia, Europe, and North America
Habitat: Fields, forests, roadsides, and stream banks

FUN FACT
Another common name for bonfire moss is Cinderella moss.

COMMON HAIRCAP MOSS
(POLYTRICHUM COMMUNE)

The common haircap moss is a dark-green moss species that grows in moist, coniferous forests. It's a low-growing plant that spreads along the ground, forming a green, carpet-like growth. The moss's stems look like tiny bottlebrushes because they're covered in short, needle-like leaves.

HOW TO SPOT

Height: 1.5 to 6 inches (4 to 15 cm)
Stem: Herbaceous
Leaves: Tiny, spine-like leaves; 0.25 to 0.4 inches (0.6 to 1 cm) long
Range: Asia, Australia, Europe, and North America
Habitat: Moist, coniferous forests

WHAT ARE MOSSES?

Mosses are tiny plants that can look like green carpets growing across forest floors or over rocks. Mosses are land plants that reproduce using spores instead of seeds. They don't have roots, but they do have stems and leaves. There are at least 12,000 moss species.

PINCUSHION MOSS
(LEUCOBRYUM GLAUCUM)

Pincushion moss is an evergreen moss that grows throughout North America and Europe. As an evergreen moss, it remains green year-round. It resembles the object its name suggests: a pincushion. The moss grows in a dense, green mound in shady areas of forests, bluffs, and even city parks. Pincushion mosses are made up of tiny stems and blade-shaped leaves. The moss ranges in color from gray-green to bright yellowish green.

HOW TO SPOT

Height: 0.5 to 5 inches (1.3 to 12.7 cm)
Stem: Herbaceous
Leaves: Tiny, blade-shaped leaves; 0.1 to 0.3 inches (0.25 to 0.76 cm) long
Range: Europe and North America
Habitat: Rocky forests, wooded bluffs, roadsides, and urban parks

SPLENDID FEATHER MOSS
(HYLOCOMIUM SPLENDENS)

The splendid feather moss is a common moss species in the northern parts of the northern hemisphere—it even grows in the Arctic. Splendid feather mosses look like ferns because their branches and tiny leaves appear frond- or feather-like. These plants grow in large patches and can form dense mats on the ground.

FUN FACT
In the United Kingdom, splendid feather moss is called glittering wood moss.

HOW TO SPOT

Height: 4 to 6 inches (10 to 15 cm)
Stem: Herbaceous
Leaves: Small frond- or feather-like leaves; 0.07 to 0.11 inches (0.17 to 0.27 cm) long
Range: Africa, Asia, Australia, Europe, New Zealand, North America, and the Caribbean
Habitat: Forests and tundra

LIVERWORTS

FLOATING CRYSTALWORT
(RICCIA FLUITANS)

The floating crystalwort is a type of liverwort. Instead of stems or leaves, floating crystalworts are made up of plant tissues called thalli. The thalli look like green stems with many Y-shaped branches. Floating crystalworts can form large colonies that float in freshwater habitats with still water, such as ponds and lakes. They may also survive underwater. Floating crystalworts don't produce flowers or seeds.

HOW TO SPOT

Stem: None
Leaves: None
Range: Europe, Asia, and North America
Habitat: Ponds, lakes, swamps, and ditches

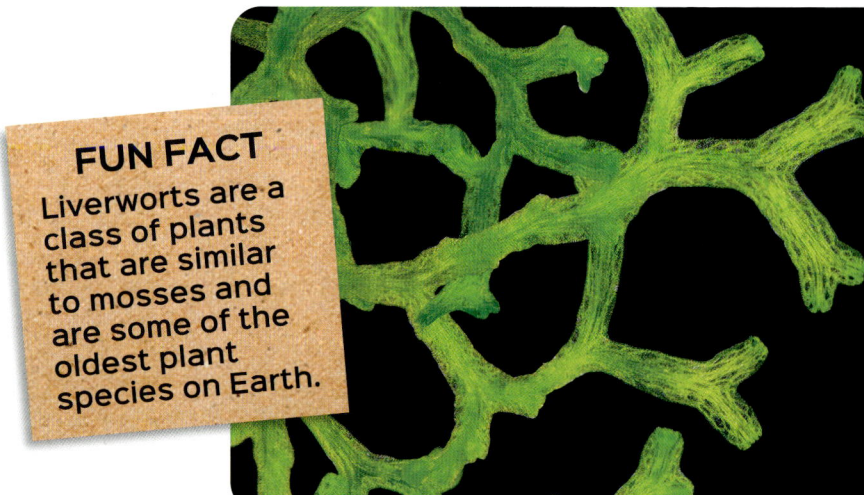

FUN FACT
Liverworts are a class of plants that are similar to mosses and are some of the oldest plant species on Earth.

UMBRELLA LIVERWORT
(MARCHANTIA POLYMORPHA)

Umbrella liverworts are commonly found clinging to wet rocks or forming large, green mats on the ground. Like other liverworts, these plants don't have stems or leaves. Instead, umbrella liverworts are made up of rosette-shaped thalli. Sometimes umbrella liverworts sprout growths that look like tiny umbrellas or palm trees. These growths are how liverworts reproduce.

HOW TO SPOT

Stem: None
Leaves: None
Range: Worldwide, from the Arctic to tropical climates
Habitat: Freshwater habitats and on wet rocks

GLOSSARY

basal
Leaves that grow from the base of a plant, often growing in a circle.

brackish
Water that is slightly salty, such as when seawater and river water mix.

compound leaf
A leaf that has many different leaflets attached to one stem.

conifer
A tree with cones and needle-like leaves; often an evergreen.

cultivar
A specific variety of plant developed by people.

deciduous
Trees that drop their leaves at least once a year, often in fall or winter.

disturbed area
A place where the topsoil has been removed or the natural habitat has been dramatically changed.

invasive
A species that is introduced to a new area and causes damage to the habitat.

leaflet
A smaller leaf that's a part of a larger compound leaf.

perennial
A plant that lives for several years.

photosynthesis
The process used by plants to convert sunlight into usable energy.

rosette
A cluster of leaves or petals that grow in a circle.

serrated
Having a jagged, saw-like edge.

spikelet
One of the small, spike-shaped flowers that make up a larger spike-shaped flower cluster.

stamen
The male, pollen-producing part of a flower.

temperate climate
A moderate climate that doesn't have temperature extremes.

TO LEARN MORE

FURTHER READINGS

Debbink, Andrea. *Trees*. Abdo, 2021.

Jose, Sarah. *Trees, Leaves, Flowers & Seeds: A Visual Encyclopedia of the Plant Kingdom*. DK, 2019.

Romero, Libby. *Wildflowers*. National Geographic, 2018.

ONLINE RESOURCES

To learn more about flowers and plants, please visit **abdobooklinks.com** or scan this QR code. These links are routinely monitored and updated to provide the most current information available.

PHOTO CREDITS

Cover Photos: iStockphoto, front (aloe vera), front (wisteria), front (cloudberries), front (sacred lotus), front (wild strawberries), back (purple coneflower), back (passion fruit); Shutterstock Images, front (bread wheat), back (black-eyed Susan); Valentyn Volkov/iStockphoto, front (chicory); Wulan Rohmawati/Shutterstock Images, front (white water lily); Nedim Bajramovic/Shutterstock Images, front (common houseleek); Deanna Oliva Kelly/Shutterstock Images, front (Venus flytrap)

Interior Photos: iStockphoto, 1 (black-eyed Susan), 1 (common lilac), 5 (bottom right), 8, 9 (bottom), 13, 14 (left), 17 (bottom), 19, 22 (left), 29 (bottom), 30, 33, 34, 40 (top), 40 (bottom), 41, 44, 45 (right), 46 (top), 52, 53 (top), 57 (top), 60 (bottom), 63 (bottom), 67 (top), 67 (bottom), 68 (top), 69, 73, 76 (top), 76 (bottom), 77, 78 (top), 81 (bottom), 82 (left), 82 (right), 84, 85 (top), 86, 90, 92 (top), 94 (top), 99 (bottom), 106 (bottom), 112 (American cranberry); Shutterstock Images, 1 (common mullein), 4 (right), 5 (top left), 5 (bottom left), 6, 7, 10, 11, 20 (top), 23, 24 (top), 26 (left), 27 (bottom), 35 (bottom), 39 (top), 42 (bottom), 43, 45 (left), 47 (bottom), 54 (top), 57 (bottom), 61 (top), 61 (bottom), 62, 64, 65 (top), 65 (bottom), 71, 74 (top), 74 (bottom), 75 (right), 78 (bottom), 83 (top), 91, 96, 97 (top), 98, 101 (bottom), 102 (top), 103, 112 (morning glory), 112 (yellow pitcher plant); Le Do/Shutterstock Images, 1 (lily of the valley), 68 (bottom); Mark Brandon/Shutterstock Images, 1 (sky plant), 32; Avalon Studio/iStockphoto, 4 (left), 5 (top right), 9 (top), 49; Nick Kurzenko/iStockphoto, 4 (middle), 50 (top); Iurii Garmash/iStockphoto, 5 (top middle), 70 (top); Alvin E. Staffan/Science Source, 6–7 (top), 27 (top); Lotus Images/Shutterstock Images, 6–7 (bottom), 26 (right), 112 (sacred lotus); Hariani Rahayu/Shutterstock Images, 12; Andrea Meling/iStockphoto, 14 (right); Peter Turner Photography/Shutterstock Images, 15; Bob Gibbons/Alamy, 16; Floral Images/Alamy, 17 (top); Ian Redding/iStockphoto, 18 (left); Victoria Tucholka/Shutterstock Images, 18 (right); Ruki Media/Shutterstock Images, 20 (bottom); Holly Guerrio/Shutterstock Images, 21; James Elkington/iStockphoto, 22 (right); Gabriele Grassl/iStockphoto, 24 (bottom); Esa Hiltula/iStockphoto, 25; Holly Guerrio/iStockphoto, 28 (top); Gerry Bishop/Shutterstock Images,

28 (bottom); Christian Ader/iStockphoto, 29 (top); Jaroslava V./Shutterstock Images, 31 (top); Christian Vinces/Shutterstock Images, 31 (bottom); Dominic Gentilcore PhD/Shutterstock Images, 35 (top); N. Nehring/iStockphoto, 36 (top); Bozhena Melnyk/Shutterstock Images, 36 (bottom); Gary Kavanagh/iStockphoto, 37; Nedim Bajramovic/Shutterstock Images, 38; Svetlana Klaise/Shutterstock Images, 39 (bottom); Milan Vachal/Shutterstock Images, 42 (top); Ksenia Lada/Shutterstock Images, 46 (bottom); Martin Fowler/Shutterstock Images, 47 (top); Waldemar Seehagen/iStockphoto, 48 (top); Artesia Wells/iStockphoto, 48 (bottom); SHS Photography/iStockphoto, 50 (bottom); Martin Wahlborg/iStockphoto, 51; Meindert van der Haven/iStockphoto, 53 (bottom); Sergey Kohl/Shutterstock Images, 54 (bottom); Picture This Images/Shutterstock Images, 55; Oscar Cadejo/iStockphoto, 56; Nancy J. Ondra/Shutterstock Images, 58; Mark Baldwin/Shutterstock Images, 59; Viktor Kitaykin/iStockphoto, 60 (top); Andrei Sitnikov/iStockphoto, 63 (top); Jane McIlroy/Shutterstock Images, 66; Khlong Wang Chao/iStockphoto, 70 (bottom); Steffen Hauser/botanikfoto/Alamy, 72; Picture Partners/Shutterstock Images, 75 (left); Vadym Zaitsev/Shutterstock Images, 79; Alexander Denisenko/iStockphoto, 80; Yves Dery/iStockphoto, 81 (top); Grigorii Pisotckii/iStockphoto, 83 (bottom); Ralf Blechschmidt/iStockphoto, 85 (bottom); Gail Jankus/Science Source, 87 (top); Nadya So/iStockphoto, 87 (bottom); Jonathan O'Rourke/Alamy, 88; Zeljko Vranjkovic Shutterstock Images, 89; Paul Bein/iStockphoto, 92 (bottom); Kuttelvaserova Stuchelova/Shutterstock Images, 93; Liudmyla Liudmyla/iStockphoto, 94 (bottom); Miroslav Hlavko/Shutterstock Images, 95; Gardens by Design/Shutterstock Images, 97 (bottom); Przemyslaw Muszynsk/Shutterstock Images, 99 (top), 107 (top); Manfred Ruckszio/Shutterstock Images, 100; Mark Heighes/Shutterstock Images, 101 (top); Henri Koskinen/Shutterstock Images, 102 (bottom); Ihor Hvozdetskyi/Shutterstock Images, 104; Duncan Shaw/Science Source, 105; Chonlasub Woravichan/Shutterstock Images, 106 (top); Ian Redding/Shutterstock Images, 107 (bottom)

ABDOBOOKS.COM
Published by Abdo Publishing, a division of ABDO, PO Box 398166, Minneapolis, Minnesota 55439. Copyright © 2022 by Abdo Consulting Group, Inc. International copyrights reserved in all countries. No part of this book may be reproduced in any form without written permission from the publisher. Abdo Reference™ is a trademark and logo of Abdo Publishing.

102021
012022

Editor: Alyssa Sorenson
Series Designer: Colleen McLaren
Content Consultant: Sarah Chamberlain, MS, Curator, The Pennsylvania State University Herbarium

Library of Congress Control Number: 2021941714
Publisher's Cataloging-in-Publication Data
Names: Debbink, Andrea, author.
Title: Flowers and plants / by Andrea Debbink
Description: Minneapolis, Minnesota : Abdo Publishing, 2022 | Series: Field guides | Includes online resources and index.
Identifiers: ISBN 9781532196959 (lib. bdg.) | ISBN 9781098218768 (ebook)
Subjects: LCSH: Flowers--Juvenile literature. | Plants--Juvenile literature. | Vegetation--Juvenile literature. | Field guides--Juvenile literature.
Classification: DDC 582--dc23